Revelation
through
Relationship

Revelation through Relationship

through

Relationship

Powerful Insights for Gaining Supernatural Revelation
and Cultivating Spiritual Intimacy with God

CORNELIA C. ARMSTRONG

Xulon Press
2301 Lucien Way #415
Maitland, FL 32751
407.339.4217
www.xulonpress.com

Paperback ISBN-13: 978-1-66283-322-9
Ebook ISBN-13: 978-1-66283-323-6

TABLE OF CONTENTS

Acknowledgments. vii

Introduction. ix

1   In The Beginning. 1

2   God Inspired Or My Desire. 9

3   Salvation - So Now That I am Saved,
    What's Next?. 15

4   Relationship - Put Your Time In 21

5   Revelation 45

6   The Essential Ingredient Fireproof Faith 59

7   The Spirit Of Agreement. 77

8   The Worship Factor. 83

9   Natural Intimacy 93

10 Spiritual Intimacy .101

11 Revelation Through Relationship Prayers. . .119

   •   Conclusion. 127

   •   About The Author 131

   •   Reference. 133

ACKNOWLEDGMENTS

I'd like to thank my Lord and Savior, Jesus Christ, for trusting me to write this book. It has taken a number of years to complete, however, I am so grateful that He chose me for this assignment. I would like to thank my husband. He has been so encouraging and helpful during this process. To my son, whom I love with my entire heart, thank you for believing in your mom, being patient with me and standing with me over the years.

Finally, I would like to thank all of my spiritual fathers, pastor friends, and spiritual leaders who taught, inspired, prayed, rebuked, encouraged, and led me throughout my Christian Journey. Specifically, I would like to acknowledge my former pastor and bishop, Benjamin Gibert who is now deceased. He encouraged me and admonished me to be obedient to the charge God had given me regarding ministry and completing this book was this, "Stay in Faith" and "Don't Stop." I am eternally grateful for his teaching and leadership.

That ye be not slothful, but followers of
them who through faith and patience
inherit the promises
Hebrews 6:12 KJV

INTRODUCTION

B ecause we were created in the image of God, our souls naturally long to be connected or reconnected to a source, something greater than ourselves. This can be compared to a newborn baby—once it has left the comfort of the mother's womb, it will long for that comfort once again. It has been said, "If you feel connected to something larger than yourself, you're driven by the very highest level of achievement, greater than the people around you, whether that means God, spirituality, or a set of values you live by." In short, something that will outlast and outlive you.

As Christians, it is important for us to be connected internally (spiritually) and externally (naturally) with God our Creator. I read an article that was published in CBN entitled, Get Connected to God, written by Nina Keegan. This put this concept into a clear, precise perspective for me.

"As we move through our busy, hectic lives driven by our calendars and "to do" lists.

We realize the importance we have placed on technology to pull us along and keep us gripped to our everyday schedules, our cell phones and computers require charging and plugging into a power source. We need cell towers, data plans, internet providers, power surge protectors, fire walls, and secure passwords and that's just to be able to be linked to everyone and everything immediately. Have you ever thought about how much trust and reliance we place in these devices to run our lives?"

"I am the vine, ye are the branches: He that abideth in me, and I in him, the same bringeth forth much fruit: for without me ye can do nothing"
John 15:5

Jesus says that being spiritually connected is like being attached to a vine. You're not going to have any fruitfulness or productivity in your life if you're out there on your own. You've got to stay connected. In plants, a disconnected branch can't bear fruit. You, as the branch, will not have the support, you will begin to wither and die. You will not have any productivity in your life if you're not spiritually connected.

"What if we stay plugged in and connected to our Creator with the same unmatched enthusiasm? What if we were to give God the same dedication, reliance, and trust that we give to these things? Would we not have the most amazing life if we started our days supercharged in the Lord and completely connected to the ultimate of all power sources? The connection that is always reliable, the one that is never subject to error, the one that can't break down or become obsolete. The one source that can never be hacked, breached, or compromised! The highly functional, trustworthy, super-intelligent, miraculous, omniscient kind of connection that can irrefutably never fail!

> God is the power source and by us being the branches, stemming from the vine, we are plugged into God and we become fully functional as a result.

> We, as humans and children of God, require the recharging that we get from being connected to our very own Creator, in the same way that a lamp must be plugged into an outlet in order for it to produce light. Without a power source, what good is a lamp? It is just a useless piece of metal glass and wire incapable of functioning in the purpose for which it was created.

Likewise what good are we? What purpose are we serving if we aren't plugged into our power source every day? We need to remain connected to the Lord to work properly and in the direction of our divine purpose through Him. We also need to be a light! Without our source, we too will be a broken lamp in the darkness."

Stay fully connected to the divine love and wisdom of our heavenly Father by wholeheartedly trusting in Him. By praying, reading the Word, and following His deep and divine purpose for your life, you will stay rooted in Him. Worship Him and surrender your days to Jesus Christ. Without Him we can do nothing, we are nothing. Like a branch pruned from the vine, it will surely die.

Stay connected to God and LIVE!

The intent of this book is to encourage and empower the reader to embrace their desire to have a deeper, connected, fulfilling relationship with God. Further, it was written for the reader to ensure and understand that true revelation from God the Father only comes through relationship and spiritual intimacy. In these pages, both the newly saved Christian and those who have been Christians for some time will find basic scriptural foundations and principles that will bring clarity and understanding regarding the following questions:

- What is Godly revelation?
- How do I develop a closer relationship with God?
- How do I maintain a relationship with God?
- What is spiritual intimacy?

It is my hope that those who read these pages will find an understanding regarding how to diligently seek God daily, principles to apply regarding developing Christ-like character that will last a lifetime. In a day when many in the body of Christ are seeking answers regarding the spiritual and natural attacks they are experiencing from the enemy, it is important to understand how to combat the deception of the enemy. Also, it is most important that believers regain the hunger and sincere desire to strive for true revelation, relationship, and closer intimacy with the true and Living God.

After many years of meditation, prayer, reading, research, and personal growth regarding this topic, the Lord gave me clear revelation on how to unfold His plan regarding developing revelation through relationship and spiritual intimacy with Him during this season. I obeyed God regarding His will, His calling, and His purpose for my life in this season. It is my heart's desire that believers and non-believers will read this writing and use it as a tool to assist them in developing a revelatory relationship with the Father and His Son, Jesus Christ. It is also my hope that the kingdom of God will be advanced and all who read this book will use the biblical principles, examples, and processes mentioned throughout each of these pages to increase in every area of their spiritual journey. Finally, it is my prayer that those who read these pages will forever, be encouraged, be inspired, and be empowered.

CHAPTER 1

IN THE BEGINNING…

*And God said, Let us make man in our
image, after our likeness: and let them have
dominion over the fish of the sea, and over
the fowl of the air, and over the cattle, and
over all the earth, and over every creeping
thing that creepeth upon the earth.
So God created man in his own image, in
the image of God created he him;
male and female created he them.*

*And God blessed them, and God said unto
them, Be fruitful, and multiply, and replenish
the earth, and subdue it: and have dominion
over the fish of the sea, and over the fowl
of the air, and over every living thing that
moveth upon the earth.*
Genesis 1: 26-28

A dam and Eve were created in the image of God, and they communed with God and had a supernatural relationship with God. Nowhere do we read of God's conversing with the trees, the fish, or the oceans. Nowhere do we see God seeking out a relationship with any of His creation, except for man, which the Bible states were created in His own image. God revealed the following in the beginning: Himself to man, His character, His wishes, and His ways. Adam and Eve responded to God divide purpose with wonder, love, and obedience. There was no fear, for there was perfect love between God and man. There was no shame; Adam and Eve were delighted to know and to be obedient to the will of God. In the beginning, they welcomed the presence and the voice of God. Their relationship with God was the reason for their very existence.

Do you remember the Prego spaghetti sauce commercial? Their slogan was "It's in there." Well, just as all the ingredients are needed to make Prego's sauce taste satisfying to the tongue, we have what we need *inside us* to receive supernatural insight and revelation from God. When God created Adam, his body was without life until God breathed His life into Adam. This lifeless body came alive, a living soul was created in the image and likeness of God.

"For as many as are led by the Spirit of God,
they are the sons of God."
Rom. 8:14

He wants all of His children to be sensitive and obedient to His voice as He leads and guides each of our lives. The Word of God lets us know that all who are led by the Spirit of God are the sons of God. The term *sons* indicate a level of maturity and intimacy in our relationship with Him. God is not looking for spiritual robots—He wants *sons*. He doesn't want us all just following a bunch of rules for the sake of obedience.

In the Old Testament, we read about the Mosaic Covenant between God and Moses. There were all kinds of rules to follow and sacrifices to make to atone for the act of sin. However, under this covenant, the people's sins were merely "covered" by the blood of the animal sacrifice. In the New Covenant, Jesus is the sacrifice for our sins. Our sins are completely washed away and removed from us so that we are now free to obey God simply because we love Him. Because of His sacrifice, we can trust and know that everything He instructs us to do is for our good. It's no longer about a long list of rules and regulations**.**

The greatest blessing we can experience on earth is a relationship with God. The first step to developing a relationship with God is to confess your sins, accept Him as your Lord and Savior. You'll realize that the life that He promises can never be found in another human. *We need Him.* A true relationship with God is developed over time and comes through following the direction of the Holy Spirit. We must allow God, by His Spirit, to take the lead.

God created man for a relationship with Himself

It is so fascinating to me that the Creator of the universe and the Creator of everything within the universe desires to fellowship and have a covenant relationship with temporal, humans—ordinary men and women.

> *"When I consider your heavens,*
> *the work of your fingers ... what is man that*
> *you are mindful of him, the son of man that*
> *you care for him?"*
> ***Ps. 8:3-4***

Although men and women are natural beings we are very much spiritual beings. We are more spiritual beings than we are natural. As a matter of fact, the spirit that dwells inside us was placed there by God.

His Spirit gives us the ability to achieve spiritual matters, and accomplish our God-given purpose on the earth. We know that we are three-part beings, just as God is triune, we are comprised of body, soul, and spirit. Our human bodies seek the natural and worldly things of the world. The soul or inner man is the place that God dwells and where we are created in His likeness. God's Word feeds our spirit and makes us aware of His presence and enables us to communicate and be in a relationship with our Father God. So we are never far away from our Creator. He created us in His image and likeness. He never walks away from us, however, we sometimes walk away from Him. Our God loves us and desires to be in close relationship with us, and His hands are always outstretched to receive us once again when we decide to return to Him.

> *"If any hear my voice and open the door,*
> *I will come into their house and eat with*
> *them, and they will eat with me."*
> ***Rev. 3:20***

He wants us to recognize His voice, open the door, and invite Him in. Once inside, He is more than willing to fellowship with us ONE TO ONE. You see, He will not come to our home, pound on the door, demand we let Him in, and then start commanding we do certain things—or else. He comes to us as a friend with a desire to engage in a relationship with Him. God so greatly wants a close relationship with those who believe and love Him. The word of God tells us that Abraham was called *a friend of God* because of the relationship that Abraham had with the Father.

"And the LORD said, 'Shall I hide from Abraham the thing which I do"...
"For I know Him, that he will command his children and his house after him, and they shall keep the way of the Lord, to do justice and judgment."
Genesis 18:17, 19

Ye are my friends, if ye do whatsoever I command you. Henceforth I call you not servants; for the servant knoweth not what his lord doeth: but I have called you friends; for all things that I have heard of my Father I have made known unto you. Ye have not chosen me, but I have chosen you, and ordained you, that ye should go and bring forth fruit, and that your fruit should remain: that whatsoever ye shall ask of the Father in my name, he may give it you. These things I command you, that ye love one another.
John 15:14-17

God wants to be in a relationship with us, He desires to reveal supernatural revelation to us in purpose, planning, and process in our everyday life. He desires to have a level of intimacy and involvement that produces a relationship that is undeniable to the world and brings glory to the Father.

CHAPTER 2

GOD INSPIRED OR MY DESIRE

S o often believers confuse the voice of God with their own imagination, thoughts, and selfish ambition. The cares of life and other outside forces fill the minds of God-fearing believers to the point in which they cannot clearly hear or discern the voice of God.

How do you discern the voice of God and how do you know that it is God speaking to you and not your own voice or imagination? How do we know when God is speaking and how do we know when we are only hearing our own thoughts and emotional desires? The Bible clearly and consistently speaks about selfish desires, both in the Old Testament to the New Testament. As believers, it is so important to understand that when we surrender our lives to Christ we begin the process of becoming new in the natural and the spiritual. We have to begin to train our flesh and allow the Spirit of God to transform our nature and our minds.

> *"For the sinful nature has its desire which is opposed to the Spirit, and the desire of the Spirit opposes the sinful nature; for these two, the sinful nature and the Spirit are in direct opposition to each other continually in conflict, so that you as believers do not always do whatever good things you want to do."*
> ### *Gal. 5:17*

Personal desire is acting on decisions according to what is pleasing you and not what God has spoken to you. When we as believers continue to display this type of behavior we do not obtain the results that God has promised us and we become frustrated with God. Things in our lives begin to go wrong, we don't get the results we feel we should have, and everything begins to fall apart. It is at this point, that we should realize that God never told us to act or move on these personal desires or individual decisions.

Years ago, after I had graduated from high school, I was attempting to figure out what was next for me and what my purpose was in life. Just like many young adults I was searching for my identity, reading books, and looking to others to figure out what type of career I should pursue. For some strange reason, I found myself enrolled at a community college attending real estate law courses. The thought of becoming a lawyer was something I'd always imaged and desired. This idea was a desire I had due to what a few family members and society conveyed I should pursue. They said that becoming a lawyer could prove to be very lucrative. However, after about six months of being required to read several real estate law books and the requirements of knowing, and remembering all of the real estate laws, I quickly realized this was not something I *desired* to pursue any longer. Another example of me acting in "my desire" happened again, this time in my early adult years. I wanted to start my own nail salon business, so I went to nail school and learned how to correctly and effectively accomplish the art and science of nail care and design. I was very successful in my endeavor; I completed my course requirements ahead of and at the top of all my classmates. I was ready to begin the process of taking my state board exam, however, my instructor had another agenda. She for some reason felt she needed to hold me back and make me wait until others in the class had completed their core requirements.

So she would not release my transcripts or certificate of completion and because I was young and not Holy

Spirit filled at this time. My flesh exploded verbally all over that instructor. So, after that confrontation, I walked away without receiving my nail license, but I did begin my own nail business. I worked alongside another salon owner who was licensed which is allowed by the state board, I was very good at what I did and made lots of money during this time, and I was just twenty-one years of age. So, my nail business was fully operational for two years but came to an end when I began to have marital problems.

You see, at the time of my first marriage, I was eighteen years old. I chose to marry, and not because I had to get married, it was *my desire*. My desire to be married at eighteen years of age led to six years of struggling with a hard life. I learned lessons, experienced physical and emotional pain, as well as physical and mental abuse. The only good that came out of this experience was the birth of my son.

My decisions made of fleshly desire as a young adult were pleasing to me at the time. However, they did not please God. This left me with results that were not very favorable. It is so very important not to act or move *on your own personal desires* when making important life-changing decisions or spiritual decisions. While I was going through the season of struggle during my young adult life, I would often pray to God and ask why He had allowed this to happen, and why had He not stopped me from getting married at such a young age?

The answer that I found to these questions was in an article I read many years later. It spoke about our free will and our life choices. You see, the challenge for most of us is that we do not want to *surrender our will* to God. The article made a great point regarding this topic.

Don Henson, wrote an article that was published in Life Hope & Truth entitled, "Free Will: What Is it?" It states the following:

> "God could have made us like machines. Machines do what they're supposed to do without thinking about doing anything different or considering why they do whatever they do. Sure, they eventually break down because they're mechanical devices. But they don't make bad choices that damage themselves or hurt other machines. Maybe the world would be a better place if people were more like machines. Then again, machines have no character, soul, or personality. Machines can't experience joy, anticipation, or pleasure. They aren't creative, spontaneous, or inquisitive.

Lacking self-awareness or consciousness, no sense of priorities and can't make plans for the future and experience the satisfaction of accomplishment. They have no relationships.

Instead of creating machines or robots, God created people. And He gave us free will—the ability to think, reason, and make our own choices. He gives us directions and instructions that show us how He wants us to live, but He allows us to decide whether we will obey. He created us with free will for a simple reason: He wants a relationship with all his children. In order to fulfill a relationship with our Lord, it is necessary for us, as believers to—Surrender our will to fulfill the purpose of God's Kingdom."

"There is a way that seems right to a man
and appears straight before him,
But its end is the way of death."
Prov. 14

CHAPTER 3

SALVATION - SO NOW THAT I AM SAVED, WHAT'S NEXT?

M ost churches express to new converts that they are now welcomed to the family of God! They're encouraged to find a local church where they can be baptized and grow in the knowledge of God through His Word, the Bible. This is all true and necessary. However, it goes much deeper than this. So many people have been deceived by the world to such a degree that revelation from God is something that happens automatically upon the conversion experience. It is my belief that revelation from God is a gift that God entrusts upon any believer who surrenders their life wholly to God. God reveals Himself to those who, of their own free will, have faith in Him. You must choose to repent, confess, and believe that Jesus is the Son of God and that He came into the world, died was buried, then rose again. He will return again.

FAITH

The original origin of faith for most believers starts at the confession of Jesus Christ as Lord and Savior. Faith is the foundational principle required and necessary for every newborn again believer of Jesus Christ. When we first made the conscious decision to confess Jesus Christ, we were charged to make the following confession.

PRAYER OF SALVATION

Lord Jesus, I know that I am a sinner, and I ask for Your forgiveness. I believe You died for my sins and rose from the dead. I turn from my sins and invite You to come into my heart and my life, for the rest of life. Father, I thank You for Your Son, Jesus. I believe that He came and died and rose again just for me. I trust and believe that His blood washes me and cleanses me from all guilt, shame, and sin. I open my heart and receive You now as my Lord and Savior and I commit myself to live my life according to Your word, Your will, and Your way. In Jesus' name, Amen.

REPENT: APOLOGIZE AND WALK AWAY

When we pray the prayer of salvation, we're admitting that we've sinned. As the Bible says, everyone has sinned except Jesus Christ. *"For all have sinned, and fall short of the glory of God" (Rom. 3:23).*

To sin is simply to fall short of the mark, as an arrow that does not quite hit the bull's eye. The prayer of salvation, then, recognizes that Jesus Christ is the only human who ever lived without sin. *"For He made Him who knew no sin to be sin for us, that we might become the righteousness of God in Him" (2 Cor. 5:21).*

After repentance, it is important to turn in the opposite direction and change anything that is in contrast to the lifestyle that the Word of God requires for every born-again believer.

CONFESS: SAY SOMETHING

When we pray the prayer of salvation, we're letting God know we believe His Word is true. By the faith He has given us, we choose to believe in Him. The Bible tells us that *"Without faith it is impossible to please Him, for he who comes to God must believe that He is, and that He is a rewarder of those who diligently seek Him" (Heb. 11:6).*

So, when we pray, asking God for the gift of salvation, we're exercising our free will to recognize that we believe in Him. This shows God that we have freely chosen to live for Him.

BELIEVE: EMBRACE WHAT YOU SAID

We acknowledge that Jesus Christ is God; that He came to earth as a man in order to live the sinless life that we cannot live; that He died in our place so that we would not have to pay the penalty we deserve.

We confess our past life of sin, living for ourselves and not obeying God.

We admit we are ready to trust Jesus Christ as our Lord and Savior.

We ask Jesus to come into our heart, take up residence there, and fill us with His Holy Spirit and begin living through us and directing our lives daily.

> *"For God so loved the world that He gave His only begotten Son, that whoever believes in Him should not perish but have everlasting life."*
> ***John 3:16***

Confession of Salvation is a gift from God and a declaration to the world and our enemy Satan that,

God the Father, His Son Jesus Christ, and the Word of God are the only True Spiritual Authorities in the life of any believer. Faith to believe in God for salvation is necessary and foundational in the life of every Christian believer. However, foundational faith can only carry you so far. So what is the answer to the question, "Now that I am saved, and a believer… what happens next to ensure that I develop a deeper relationship with God?" This question can be answered in one word, "Pursuit."

Other words that relate to the word pursuit are, follow, chase, tag, shadow, tail, trace, track, and hunt. These words can be applied to the actions that every believer must take to gain a deeper revelation of who God is and grow in a closer relationship with God. This pursuit for any believer requires that you mature to the next level of Faith. At this level, adequate time must be put in to obtain a lasting and eternal result. *"Blessed are* they which do hunger and thirst after righteousness: for they shall be filled." *(Matt. 5:6)*.

CHAPTER 4

RELATIONSHIP - PUT YOUR TIME IN

W hen you're in a relationship you live to please the object of your affection. A relationship is not about you it is about the one that you seek to please and grow into a deeper relationship with. The root word of relationship is *relate*.

Webster's dictionary defines the word relate as *to connect with, link up, correlate with, have a rapport with, respond to, sympathize with, feel sympathy for, identify with, empathize with, connect with, understand, speak the same language as, be in tune with,* and *be on the same wavelength with.*

So it is with our Father God and His Son Jesus Christ. If we say we love Him, then we must live a lifestyle that depicts these characteristics. The life you live after you confess that you are a follower of Christ is no longer just about you, it is about developing a relationship with the one you say you have surrendered to. Having a relationship is not a religious experience and revelation of who God is and cannot be obtained until there is a true relationship between you and Jesus Christ.

So how is this done? How does one develop a relationship with Jesus Christ? The answer to that question is, "Put your time in." The following are a few key elements of "Putting your time in" and developing a deeper relationship with Jesus Christ:

- **Cultivate Your Vertical Relationship**
- **Live A Consecrated Life**
- **Embrace The Mind Of Christ**
- **Develop A Fervent Prayer Life**

CULTIVATE YOUR VERTICAL RELATIONSHIP

In life, we know that relationships are important, and you cannot avoid them, therefore it is necessary to become aware of the various types of relationships that we as humans encounter daily. First, we must know and understand that any successful relationship requires time and effort. So having stated this, the question arises, what should be the most important relationship in a believer's life?

The most important relationship man will ever encounter is his relationship with God. Man was designed with an inner hunger to *know* God. Man was created by God to his Creator and enjoy an intimate relationship with Him. Prior to the fall of man, God and man walked together in the garden; see Genesis 3:8.

God didn't just create man to rule over him, He intended to have a relationship between Himself and the man he made in His image. Having relationships between God and His children was something God has desired from the beginning. Relationships can be placed into two types of categories, *vertical and horizontal*. The vertical relationship is the relationship between God and man. The horizontal relationship is the relationship we have with each other, for example, mother and daughter, husband, and wife, sister, and brother, etc. The Word of God states, *"If a man say, I love God, and hateth his brother, he is a liar: for he that loveth not his brother whom he hath seen, cannot love God whom he hath not seen" (1 John 4:20).*

Love the Lord your God with all your heart and with all your soul and with all your mind. This is the first and greatest commandment. And the second is like it: Love your neighbor as yourself.' All the Law

> *and the Prophets hang on these*
> *two commandments.*
> ***Matthew 22:37-40***

The vertical relationship must always precede the horizontal relationship—otherwise, all horizontal relationships could be jeopardized.

> *As the hart panteth after the water brooks,*
> *so panteth my soul after thee Oh God...*
> ***Psalm 42:1***

My consistent way of cultivating my vertical relationship is worship. God placed this gift inside of me many years ago and I am so grateful. Meditation, confession, reading the Word, engaging with like-minded faith-filled believers are all avenues for cultivating a vertical relationship with Jesus Christ, and I diligently engage in all these aspects. However, worship has been my mainstay.

My personal worship is always directed toward God. When I direct my worship towards God, he then allows His presence, His anointing, and His revelation to dwell in and around me. During my personal time of worship, I am not concerned about my needs, wants, or desires—nor the cares of this world. My soul and spirit are at one with the Father, Son, and

Holy Spirit and I am being restored, revived, and resuscitated during my personal worship time with God. My objective during those times is to let God know how much I love Him, need Him, appreciate Him, and convey how grateful and thankful I am for Him in my life.

Vertical is a direction perpendicular to a horizontal direction which simply means: straight up and down. So when you embrace this you understand that God is in heaven we are on earth. Our communications with God are sent upward—vertical—to Him.

It has been said, "The vertical relationship is probably the most neglected relationship." Yet, it is the most important relationship that you can have because, while horizontal relationships are important, the vertical relationship produces eternal results. So what are some examples of ways that people are more careful to maintain their horizontal relationships, rather than making time for their vertical relationship with God? It is important to love are neighbors, sisters, brothers, children, husband and wives. The Word of God tells us that this is very important. This is how we show the world the love God that resides on the inside of us. However, this does not require us to allow others to take away time consistently from the time set aside for developing our vertical relationship with

God. Trust me, I am guilty of the inability to say NO, but God is counting on you to always prioritize your vertical relationship with Him. Just like everything in life we must remember to prioritize those things that have eternal consequences.

The vertical relationship grants us access into a world that cannot be seen with physical eyes, however, it is a world more powerful than the natural world in which we live. We understand and know that God has given us access to Him, but it is only through the spiritual side of our beings that we gain this access. If you only seek Him in the natural or physical, you will never develop a relationship with God. The Bible states,

> *"God is a Spirit: and they that worship him*
> *must worship him in spirit and in truth"*
> ### *John 4:24*

At the age of twenty-five, I truly gave my life to Jesus Christ. Although I had been raised in a Christ-centered home, I did not know or understand much about the God I'd heard about and learned of at church. Chapter twenty-five of my life was an awakening season for me spiritually, and I wanted everyone to know who the spiritual authority was in my life. So I purchased a gold cross, which I still own and wear to this day around my neck, to symbolize who I am, who I belong to and what I believe. This season of my life was just the beginning of developing my vertical relationship with Jesus Christ.

I read a study guide that was written by Pete Bumgarner for STC Bible College entitled, "Vertical & Horizontal Relationships." The article gave me a greater definition of the cross as it relates to the topic of cultivating a vertical relationship with Jesus Christ. It gives another example of the importance of developing a vertical relationship:

> "The cross, when we look at it we are reminded at Christian Believers that its vertical beam gives us peace with God our Father through Christ Jesus in the power of the Holy Spirit. The horizontal beam should remind us that Christ accomplished peace for us between each other and that we are commanded to walk in unity and love with other believers by the power of the Holy Spirit, for the glory of God."

> The vertical beam represents restoration, agreement, and harmony of mankind with God. The cross is a beautiful picture of reconciliation. To reconcile is to bring into agreement or harmony; make compatible or

consistent; to restore. Every time a Christian believer looks at the cross, whether it's a charm on a necklace or on the wall in a church, it's a beautiful reminder of the gift we have received and the burden we've been given. We've been called into a constant death to self in our vertical relationship with God and His will for our lives."

The knowledge of Jesus Christ sacrifice is very necessary in the life of every believer. True revelation of God and His Son, comes through Jesus sacrifice. Our relationship to the cross is both vertical and horizontal, however, the most important relationship that should constantly and consistently be developed is the vertical relationship.

THE HOLY SPIRIT

The Holy Spirit is the key that unlocks the door to receiving supernatural revelation.

The Bible tells us that the Holy Spirit is a comforter, teacher, instructor, and counselor. He is indeed all these things and more in our time of need. The only way to be led by the Spirit is to follow God's command to be filled with the Spirit.

> *"And be not drunk with wine, wherein is*
> *excess; but be filled with the Spirit..."*
> ***Eph. 5:18***

The Holy Spirit reveals why it is so important that every Christian believer desires to be filled with the Holy Spirit. Every person that confesses Jesus as their personal Lord and has a repenting heart, should desire to be led by the Spirit of God. The Bible says;

> *"But ye are not in the flesh, but in the Spirit,*
> *if so be that the Spirit of God dwell in you.*
> *Now if any man have not the Spirit of Christ,*
> *he is none of his."*
> ***Rom. 8:9***

"Howbeit when he, the Spirit of truth, is come, he will guide you into all truth: for he shall not speak of himself; but whatsoever he shall hear, that shall he speak: and he will shew you things to come."
John 16:13

We must have the Holy Spirit if we are to operate in supernatural revelation.

"Who has understood the mind of the LORD, or instructed him as his counselor?"
Isa. 40:13

EMBRACE THE MIND OF CHRIST

Having the mind of Christ means we "look at life from God's perspective, we desire His values and not those of our own. To have the mind of Christ means, I think and desire God's thoughts and I aim to please Him and Him alone. The Bible says this;

"I have been crucified with Christ; it is no longer I who live, but Christ lives in me; and the life which I now live in the flesh I live by faith in the Son of God, who loved me and gave Himself for me."
Gal. 2:20

Because of the decision each believer makes when we confess Jesus as Lord and Savior,

we make an outward declaration of inward experience regarding a new and supernatural relationship that we now have with an eternal and living God.

Once the decision to follow Christ and confession is made to denounce the ways of the world, it is most important to remember that we must daily "PUT HIM ON," the mind of Christ. Soldiers were a helmet specifically made for combat to be worn when they go into battle to protect their skull outwardly and their brain inwardly. If the skull or brain is injured in any way it affects the soldiers' ability to think and be affective on the battle field. So, it is with the Mind of Christ, we must intentionally embody, embrace, change and surrender our way of thinking and Embrace the Mind of Christ. This allows the believer to recognize, discern, understand and know how to execute the plan and purpose that God has created and place them here on earth to accomplish. Understand this, we live in a world that does not know God, and all manner of evil takes place in the world on a daily basis. We live with and interact with people who do not know or understand God, as we do. The Word of God says that:

*But the unspiritual man simply cannot
accept the matters which the Spirit deals
with—they just don't make sense to him,
for, after all, you must be spiritual to see
spiritual things. The spiritual man, on the
other hand, has an insight into the meaning
of everything, though his insight may baffle
the man of the world. This is because the
former is sharing in God's wisdom, and
'Who has known the mind of the Lord that
he may instruct him?' Incredible as it may
sound, we who are spiritual have the very
thoughts of Christ!*
1 Cor. 2: 14-16

We must recognize and understand that unbelievers
will not always understand, or agree with our beliefs,
our lifestyle our love for and in the Word of God and
His Son Jesus Christ. This must not stop us or cause
us to waver in our quest to obtain, transform our mind
to the Mind of Christ.

*Not that I have already attained, or am
already perfected; but I press on, that I
may lay hold of that for which Christ Jesus
has also laid hold of me. Brethren, I do not
count myself to have apprehended; but one
thing I do, forgetting those things which are*

*behind and reaching forward to those things
which are ahead, I press toward the goal for
the prize of the upward call of God in Christ
Jesus. Therefore let us, as many as are
mature, have this mind; and if in anything
you think otherwise, God will reveal even
this to you. Nevertheless, to the degree that
we have already attained, let us walk by the
same rule, let us be of the same mind...*
Philippians 3:12-16

When we as believers embrace the mind of Christ, we begin to understand God's plan for the world and understand that He wants to bring about His kingdom's purpose in the earth. The job or mandate of every faith leader is to move and direct the people of God from their own agenda and introduce them to God's agenda. By no means am I implying that faith leaders should manipulate or attempt to control anyone, however, through teaching, Godly counsel, and prayer this is accomplished. It is also needful for every believer to be in pursuit of the will of God for their individual lives.

The Bible states clearly:

*Therefore, I urge you, brothers and sisters,
in view of God's mercy, to offer your bodies*

as a living sacrifice, holy and pleasing to
God—this is your true and proper worship.
2 Do not conform to the pattern of this
world, but be transformed by the renewing
of your mind. Then you will be able to test
and approve what God's will is—his good,
pleasing and perfect will.
Romans 12:1-3

Therefore it is also so very important for
individuals to have the Holy Spirit inside
you. The only way to possess the Holy Spirit
comes by faith in God. "You, however, are
controlled not by the sinful nature but by the
Spirit, if the Spirit of God lives in you. And if
anyone does not have the Spirit of Christ, he
does not belong to Christ"
Rom. 8:9

After receiving salvation, it is the responsibility of
every believer to yield to the Holy Spirit's leading
and let the Spirit of God transform his/her life.
Another very key component to developing the mind
of Christ is reading the Word of God. This will allow
you begin to understand and the heart and personality
of God. As you study the scriptures the Holy Spirit
will begin to reveal who God is and what He desires
from His children.

I have found that praying before reading the Word and asking God to help me understand and apply His Word to my life, allows my spirit to receive the Word of God without hindrances. Finally, have patience, it takes time and sometimes even years to learn to hear, recognize and understand God's voice and develop the Mind of Christ. This is not something that happens overnight and comes with many tests, trials, and life challenges. Trust and know that no matter how long it takes, you can be confident in this, God is faithful and patient with those who love him and seek Him with a pure heart. He hears our prayers, and He will respond.

DEVELOP A FERVENT PRAYER LIFE

Your prayer life positions you to be in a consistent place of tuned-in living. The stronger your prayer life, the more the Holy Spirit begins to reveal the mind of Christ to you. Our prayer life *is empowered* by the Holy Spirit; it gives us the ability to receive empowerments from God, to bind and loose natural and supernatural manifestation. However, we must first understand and embrace our identity as a blood-bought and blood-washed child of God. We must also walk in the full authority of our kingdom rights and say and speak only what God reveals by the Holy Spirit. Fervent prayer is focused, bold, and cultivated in isolation and produces natural and supernatural results. The Bible states that we are to pray without ceasing, the Bible also says that men should always pray and not faint. Frequent and fervent prayer is an essential part of our relationship with God. It is faith in God and His promises that He will hear and answer us when we seek Him with clean hands and a pure heart. Also, we must pray in line with the will of God.

The Bible speaks of Elijah's fervent prayer to God, in *1Kings 17.* Elijah prayed and his focused, intense prayer teaches us several lessons regarding how fervent prayer is cultivated in isolation and produces natural and supernatural results.

Elijah was focused

Elijah learned to be completely dependent on God. After Elijah's first confrontation with King Ahab, God sent him to the Kerith Brook. There Elijah sat, no food, no provisions. But God saw his needs. It was there, with everything taken away, that God sent ravens to bring him food.

Elijah was bold

Elijah was bold. He asked with bold faith, believing that God was able. He believed that God was faithful, and that He would answer his prayers. He called on God with enough faith to believe God would answer even the most audacious prayer and, God did answer that bold prayer, He poured out His power repeatedly.

Elijah's fervent prayer cultivated and manifested supernatural results

Elijah prayed boldly for miracles. Elijah didn't waste his time with small requests to God. He went straight to the big requests. He prayed for a drought in the land, raising of the widow's son from the dead, and called down fire from heaven to consume the offering on Mount Carmel.

At the usual time for offering during the evening sacrifice, Elijah the prophet walked up to the altar and prayed, "O Lord, God of Abraham, Isaac, and Jacob, prove today that you are God in Israel and that I am your servant. Prove that I have done all this at your command. Immediately the fire of the Lord flashed down from heaven and burned up the young bull, the wood, the stones, and the dust. It even licked up all the water in the trench!
1 Kings 18:36, 38

Elijah prayed fervently until he saw the answer. Elijah knew that sometimes an answer doesn't come immediately. He knew that he must pray until he saw a breakthrough. And he was committed for the duration and his answer manifested. Another example is when Elijah climbed to the top of Mount Carmel and bowed to the ground and prayed with his face between his knees.

> *Then he said to his servant, "Go and look out toward the sea." The servant went and looked, then returned to Elijah and said, "I didn't see anything." Seven times Elijah told him to go and look. Finally the seventh time, his servant told him, "I saw a little cloud about the size of a man's hand rising from the sea." Then Elijah shouted, "Hurry to Ahab and tell him, 'Climb into your chariot and go back home. If you don't hurry, the rain will stop you!'" And soon the sky was black with clouds. A heavy wind brought a terrific rainstorm, and Ahab left quickly for Jezreel."*
> ***1 Kings 18:42b-45***

Elijah prayed the drought into existence. He began to seek God for rain. Not a little rain, but enough rain to nourish the land. He asked, no response, he asked again, still no response from God. Seven times he asked and sent his servant to look for an answer. He prayed expecting an answer. Finally, after seven times, a small cloud began to form. Even just a small signal that God had heard his prayer was enough. He knew a small signal showed God was moving in response to his prayers.

Fervent Prayer should always be aligned with the Will of God

Elijah was as human as we are, and yet when he prayed fervently that no rain would fall, none fell for three and a half years! Then, when he prayed again, the sky sent down rain and the earth began to yield its crops. What was it about Elijah that made his prayers, his life, so powerful and effective?

Elijah's prayers pointed the people back to God. Elijah was completely in tune with God. He listened for God's voice and he walked in obedience. He prayed in agreement with the Word of God. His prayers pointed the people back to God. We must pray earnestly, fervently. We must not give up. We must continually come before the Father asking Him to hear us, to answer.

We must have an attitude of expectation, believing that God is able and willing to answer our prayers. We must remember that it is God's faithfulness that we are calling on, His character. It's about a God who longs to be in relationship with us and reveal to us His will for our lives. We must remember fervent prayer is about ordinary people calling on an invincible God, to reveal to us His will and His desire. Fervent prayer reveals the will of God for our lives. We must have faith that He is willing and able to do far more than we could ever ask or imagine.

> *"Confess your trespasses to one another, and pray for one another, that you may be healed. The effective, fervent prayer of a righteous man avails much."*
> ***James 5:16***

FERVENT PRAYER MUST HAVES

1. TIME

Set aside time when your life does not require you to be obligated to anything or anyone else.

Remember, it is not how long you pray but how well you pray that matters. Insure that you set aside quality time to pray fervently. Pray until you receive a breakthrough, adequately plead your case before God. Pray until the Holy Spirit gives you peace and releases you.

2. ISOLATION

It is very necessary to STOP the noise without and the noise within, so that true fervent prayer can take place. Isolation, all around you and also within you must be in place to effectively receive answers from God. Isolation is a MUST. Hearing from God is about more than just turning off the cell phone and getting away from others. It requires a quiet spirit and mind; it means becoming still enough on the inside despite the craziness on the outside.

3. PRAY THE WORD OF GOD

God listens for His Word when we pray and God is only moved by His Word. Therefore, you have to know what the Word of God says about your current situation and remind God of what His Word says. Search the Scriptures for God's Word concerning the issue, meditate on them and then pray to God and allow Him to respond.

> *"And this is the confidence that we have in him, that, if we ask anything according to his will, he heareth us and if we know that*

he hear us, whatsoever we ask,
we know that we have the petitions that
we desired of him."
1 John 5:14-15

"Put me in remembrance:
let us plead together: declare thou,
that thou mayest be justified."
Isa. 43:26

4. FAITH

It takes strong faith to pray fervent prayers. Anyone who comes to God in prayer must first trust and know that God will answer your prayer. Faith is the ingredient that draws God's attention to your prayers, God will ONLY and ALWAYS be moved by His Word.

"But without faith it is impossible to please
him: for he that cometh to God must believe
that He is, and that He is a rewarder of them
that diligently seek Him"
Heb. 11:6

5. RIGHTEOUSNESS

We know that belief in Jesus Christ as the Son of God and Righteousness is the required lifestyle of the believer. So then if we live by this standard, we know that God sees and hears us when we pray fervently to Him. The Word of God states that His eyes are over the righteous. God sees exactly what we are going through. His ears are open unto our prayers; He sees and hears every word that we say to Him when we pray.

Just as God sees and hears the righteous when they pray, the Bible also clearly states that God cannot stay where sin is. "The face of the Lord is against them that do evil." God has to turn His face when sin enters His presence. It is only when we repent and turn from evil that God can see us and hear our fervent prayers. It is only when we pray according to His will. God may not always come when we think He should or answer our prayers the way we want Him to. We do know that He sees us and hears us and He answers us according to His Will and purpose for our lives. Trust and know that He is the creature of the universe, and He always has the better plan for our lives.

"For the eyes of the Lord are over the righteous, and his ears are open unto their prayers: but the face of the Lord is against them that do evil."
1 Pet. 3:12

CHAPTER 5

REVELATION

B y definition, *revelation* is the uncovering, a removal of the veil, and a disclosure of what was previously unknown. Revelation is God's manifestation of Himself to humankind in such a way that men and women can know, fellowship, have understanding, and be in relationship with Him.

> *"Blessed are you, Simon son of Jonah, for this was not revealed to you by man, but by my Father in heaven."*
> **Matt. 16:17**

The knowledge of who Jesus is cannot be attained through human efforts, it comes through having a relationship with God. Revelation of God *reveals* evidence.

4501 Herbert Street

At five years old, my family and I lived on Herbert Street in Detroit, MI. This is where I first experienced a supernatural encounter with God. I could say many things about growing up in this large building on Herbert Street and how it has shaped and affected parts of my life today. However, this is not the time to dwell on such things. You see, when I was a young child living in this old apartment building, I didn't know then (but I do know now), that God was always with me. There were several units in this building and we lived on the first floor. The homes were made up of three small to medium-sized units. The unit that my mother and father used as their bedroom had a very large closet that was made up of cement blocks covered with cement and painted with dark gray paint. I remember that it was always very cold in their closet. It was not only cold but also very dark.

One small window hung on the back wall of the closet. Illogically, it perched too high on the wall to be useful. The tiny hint of outdoors was far above the clothes rack. I remember retreating to this closet many times during my childhood. The closet was my escape from the harsh sounds of angry words, arguments, and physical altercations between my father and mother. On occasion, I'd find myself in this cold closet during the late-night hours. You, see when the loud noises started, it usually happened when my father came home. He'd drink all evening and into such late hours that it would soon be early morning. All, of these events happened before my father was delivered from alcohol. I vividly remember the times I'd sit in that small space for hours. Wide awake, I stared into that small window. It seemed as if I was drawn in by the light that shined through that very small window located at the top of the back closet wall. The light that brought a new day, hopefully, filled with peace, silence, and safety. I remember how bright and beautiful the light was that shined through the small window. It was warm and comforting and it made me feel safe. Sometimes I would fall asleep on the cold floor of the closet. I know now, as a spirit-filled believer that, as a child, I was in the manifested presence of God. God's presence was so strong but yet so gentle. Everything seemed so clear to me. I remember God speaking to me. He'd tell me, "You're special, I made you different from the others, you are safe, and you will do great things."

Although 4501 Herbert Street is now a vacant lot, the building having been torn down long ago, the experience—the revelation and relationship that began there cannot and will not ever be denied. The Bible says that we must come to God with a pure heart. With childlike faith, we receive Him and also receive His revelation of who He is and what He has called us to accomplish during our time here on earth. I'm so grateful and elated that He counted me worthy at a very young age to reveal Himself to me in this way. I came to Him with my childlike faith and He ever so gently ushered me into His presence. He began to reveal and draw me into relationship with Him in so many ways that I am still experiencing and benefiting from today.

And calling to him a child, he put him in the
midst of them and said, "Truly, I say to you,
unless you turn and become like children,
you will never enter the kingdom of heaven.
Whoever humbles himself like this child is the
greatest in the kingdom of heaven."
Matthew 18:2-4

TYPES OF REVELATION

Natural Revelation

Most humans living on the planet recognize or have the revelation of God. Some might say a *higher power*. How, do we know this? We know because God has revealed Himself in one way or another in every aspect of our lives. When God created the world He left a road map—bread crumbs, you might say—for us to recognize who He is. Natural revelation is perceived in the things that God has created.

"For ever since the world was created, people have seen the earth and sky. Through everything God made, they can clearly see his invisible qualities--his eternal power and divine nature. So they have no excuse for not knowing God."
Rom. 1:20

The heavens declare the glory of God; the skies proclaim the work of his hands. Day after day they pour forth speech; night after night they display knowledge. There is no speech or language where their voice is not heard. Their voice goes out into all the earth, their words to the ends of the world. In the heavens he has pitched a tent for the sun, which is like a bridegroom coming forth from his pavilion, like a champion rejoicing to run his course. It rises at one end of the heavens and makes its circuit to the other; nothing is hidden from its heat.
Psalm 19:1-6

Natural Revelation is God's self-disclosure of Himself in a general way to all mankind at all times.

...the living God, which made heaven,
and earth, and the sea, and all things
that are therein:
Who in times past suffered all nations to walk
in their own ways. Nevertheless
He left not Himself without witness, in that
He did good, and gave us rain from heaven,
and fruitful seasons, filling our hearts
with food and gladness.
Acts 14:-15-17

It is has been said that "Creation as a part of God's general revelation affirms certain facts about God. Nature testifies of God's existence." Nature is not fused with God, God is the creator of all natural things that exist on the earth. God communicates things about Himself through nature so that we recognize who He is and how much He loves and cares for us. We come to know more about ourselves through the natural revelation that God manifests on the earth.

Consider this:

The heavens are a sign to all mankind that God does exist; they show us a continual witness of God's existence.

The shining of the sun in the sky gives witness to the existence of God. Nothing can hide from the sun, and no man or woman can hide from God. All of heaven declares His glory from the smallest to the largest God has revealed Himself in nature. The truth about God naturally reveals itself for all to see.

Still, all of this is not enough. The revelation of God in nature is not sufficient for us to know Him. As it happened, the truth of creation and nature has been corrupted by the sin of men.

Unfortunately, many people have corrupted the general revelation of God and have chosen to worship and serve the creation rather than the Creator.

> *"Instead of worshipping the Creator, they*
> *have turned creation into 'a god.' Because*
> *they exchanged the truth about God*
> *for a lie and worshiped and served the*
> *creature rather than the Creator, who is*
> *blessed forever."*
> **Rom. 1:25**

Nature does not bring us into relationship with God. It reveals the power of God without revealing His person. We must seek more than the testimony of creation to know God in the Spirit—the supernatural realm. This is where God reveals who He is and His purpose and plan for our lives.

Supernatural Revelation

God wants to provide us with His truth and His revelation; however, it is up to us to receive it and not distort or misrepresent God's truth and His revelation. Natural Revelation is available to everyone; however, Supernatural Revelation is manifested to specific people at specific times. This type of revelation is a Gift from God.

Supernatural revelation very simply is information or insight that reveals the will of God, by God, to anointed, Holy Spirit-led believers regarding past, present, and future events.

The Word of God and the Holy Spirit work in tandem to reveal the supernatural revelation of God's perfect will. We can read the Word of God and recite the Word of God, however, without the Holy Spirit we cannot understand what Gods' perfect will is for any given situation is for the past, present, or future. The Bible says;

> *"I appeal to you therefore, brothers, by the mercies of God, to present your bodies as a*

living sacrifice, holy and acceptable to God,
which is your spiritual worship. Do not be
conformed to this world, but be transformed
by the renewal of your mind, that by testing
you may discern what is the will of God,
what is good and acceptable and perfect."
Rom. 12:1–2

The Word of God is clear and tells us that turning one's back on the world, and having one's mind renewed (by God) enables you to discern and experience God's individual will for you specifically. Supernatural revelation of God's purpose or plan has no flaws, no missing pieces. It is complete.

God is omniscient, which means He is all-knowing. He knows what He wants to accomplish in us in every season and dispensation of life. He knows what we will do, and what we will not do, in any given circumstance. Therefore, His plans for us will never fail; they will never be flawed by some missing piece of information, some unknown detail. God's plan and purpose for each and every believer is for our good and for His Glory. Our God is a relational God. If we abide in Him—the vine—then we can be assured that we will have a continual revelation of His plan and His strategies for our personal lives at this moment and what His plans are for us in the future.

> *"Unto you it is given to know the mystery of*
> *the kingdom of God."*
> **Mark 4:11**

In this scripture, Jesus is teaching a parable to His disciples and those that are also around and listening to what is being said. "Unto you it is given to know the mystery of the kingdom of God." He directly stated this to the disciples and those who are true believers that they have on the inside of them what is needed to understand and know the *mystery* of the kingdom of God. What is it that the disciples and other believers have that non-believers do not have on the inside that reveals this *mystery*? They have the Holy Spirit.

The Holy Spirit reveals the mystery of the kingdom of God. What does the mystery convey? The Holy Spirit reveals deeper insight, deeper meaning, and the mind of Christ.

Therefore, the mystery must be revealed and requires something more to comprehend. Jesus taught the *Sermon on the Mount* and spoke that, in order to *see* God, you must be pure of heart.

> *"Blessed are the pure in heart; for they*
> *shall see God."*
> **Matt. 5:8**

I have read this scripture many times and the word *see* leaps from the page. I asked myself the question, did Matthew mean *see* with the natural eye or spiritual eye? If we are pure in heart, then it must be determined that we no longer filter our lives in a natural or physical manner, but we must begin to filter everyday life occurrences through the Holy Spirit. If this is the meaning that is to be applied regarding the mystery of the kingdom of God, then one can only conclude, "for they shall *see* God," which implies to see God through the Holy Spirit. So those at the meeting were unfriendly and had a negative attitude towards Jesus. They could not understand the mystery of the kingdom of God. The scripture states:

> *Those who were with Jesus and the twelve*
> *followers came to Him when He was alone.*
> *They asked about the picture-story. He said*
> *to them, "You were given the secrets about*
> *the Holy nation of God. Everything is told*
> *in picture-stories to those who are outside*
> *the Holy nation of God. They see, but do not*
> *know what it means. They hear, but do not*
> *understand. If they did, they might turn to*
> *God and have their sins forgiven."*
> **Mark 4:10-12**

Supernatural revelation is also layered and manifested in many ways, it takes time to understand, therefore, you must be intentional in your pursuit and sincere in your desire to engage and receive supernatural revelation. Also, it is important to know and understand that supernatural revelation and prophesy are not the same. When an individual prophesies they speak and profess what God is saying. Supernatural revelation also comes from God, however, it is not always professed or prophesied to others. One common factor that they both have is that they are revealed in part and you most have the gift of the Holy Spirit dwelling on the inside to operate in either of these gifts.

> *For we know in part, and we prophesy in part. But when that which is perfect is come, then that which is in part shall be done away.... For now we see through a glass, darkly; but then face to face: now I know in part; but then shall I know even as also I am known.*
> ***1 Corinthians 13:9-10 &12***

Because prophecy and supernatural revelation come from God we expect them to be perfect. However, Paul who is the author of this passage of scripture states that they are not perfect and only revealed in part. This does not mean that the message was not from God. It only means that we can only speak prophesy or receive supernatural revelation on the level that our human flesh or nature can yield. Because we live in the flesh, or natural realm, we are prone to error. God is not to be blamed for our human errors or weaknesses. We sometimes are confused by our own desires and confuse the message that God is revealing. Again, this is why it is so important to have the gift of the Holy Spirit dwelling on the inside. The job of the Holy Spirit is to lead, guide, direct, and to provide correction and conviction when our flesh wants to produce false or imperfect results.

"But the person who is not a Christian does not understand these words from the Holy Spirit. He thinks they are foolish. He cannot understand them because he does not have the Holy Spirit to help him understand."
1 Cor. 2:14

CHAPTER 6

THE ESSENTIAL INGREDIENT
FIREPROOF FAITH

B y definition, *Fireproof Faith* is the steadfast
relentless pursuit of the true and living God.
His will, His way and His Word. Regardless of how
I feel, what I see, or what the world thinks, it is
absolute truth. This type of faith is essential in the life
of every believer. It is also necessary for the believer
to maintain a lasting relationship with God.

For I know the plans I have for you,"
declares the Lord, "plans to prosper you
and not to harm you, plans to give you hope
and a future. Then you will call on me and
come and pray to me, and I will listen to
you. You will seek me and find me when you
seek me with all your heart. I will be found
by you," declares the Lord, "and will bring
you back from captivity. I will gather you
from all the nations and places where I have

banished you," declares the Lord, "and will
bring you back to the place from which
I carried you into exile.
Jeremiah 29:11-14

FIREPROOF FAITH IS: *MATURE*

Believers who possess mature fireproof faith do not have room for doubt or disbelief in their life. This is because they realize that doubt and disbelief are real and everyone has to deal with doubt and disbelief at some point in their individual lives. However, believers who possess mature fireproof faith do not nurture the thoughts of doubt and disbelief. They have learned to rebuke doubt and disbelief from their minds. They have had many life experiences that have caused them to be placed in positions where they have had to trust God in very hard and seemingly helpless situations. However, because of their relationship and past victories with Jesus Christ, their faith is now fireproof and mature.

Maturity means that an individual has depth. Those who have depth imply that an individual has a relationship that is deeper than one can see with the eye. Their faith has been tried and now able to stand in the face of adversity. Mature believers are not idle in their faith, they do not assume God will do all the work for them when God has clearly instructed those who chose Him to abide in Him.

> *"Put out of your life hate and lying. Do not pretend to be someone you are not. Do not always want something someone else has. Do not say bad things about other people. As new babies want milk, you should want to drink the pure milk which is God's Word so you will grow up and be saved from the punishment of sin. If you have tasted of the Lord, you know how good He is."*
> **1 Peter 2**

Mature Christians are less dependent on themselves, and more dependent on the Father.

> *I am the true vine, and my Father is the gardener. Every branch in me that does not bear fruit he takes away, and every branch that does bear fruit he prunes, that it may bear more fruit. Already you are clean because of the word that I have spoken to you. Abide in me, and I in you. As the branch cannot bear fruit by itself, unless it abides in the vine, neither can you, unless you abide in me. I am the vine; you are the branches. Whoever abides in me and I in him, he it is*

*that bears much fruit, for apart from me you
can do nothing.*

*As the Father has loved me, so have I
loved you. Abide in my love. If you keep
my commandments, you will abide in
my love, just as I have kept my Father's
commandments and abide in his love. These
things I have spoken to you, that my joy may
be in you, and that your joy may be full.*

*This is my commandment, that you love one
another as I have loved you. Greater love has
no one than this that someone lay down his
life for his friends. You are my friends if you
do what I command you. No longer do I call
you servants, for the servant does not know
what his master is doing; but I have called
you friends, for all that I have heard from my
Father I have made known to you.*
John 15:1-15

Mature Christians seek to continue to grow in faith
and holiness, they do not grow more dependent on
themselves. They solely depend on Christ alone and
obedience to His command to love God and love others.
Mature Christians don't take credit for themselves, they

humbly follow Jesus Christ and His commandments and trust in the Word of God.

Mature fireproof faith believers have strong convictions; they are certain and sure that what God said in His Word is true and cannot fail. They further believe that what God says in His Word applies to them and all areas of their lives. Mature fireproof faith believers are not moved or shaken by what others say regarding their personal belief and personal relationship with Jesus Christ.

FIREPROOF FAITH IS: *INTENTIONAL*

What does it mean to be Intentional? Well to answer this question we have only to look into the Word of God that shows us that God was very intentional from the beginning of creation even unto the death of the cross.

"And God blessed them, and God said unto them, be fruitful, and multiply, and replenish the earth, and subdue it: and have dominion over the fish of the sea, and over the fowl of the air, and over every living thing that moveth upon the earth."
Genesis 1:28

*"My food," said Jesus, "is to do the will of
him who sent me and to finish his work."*
John 4:34

*"For the Son of Man came to seek and
to save the lost."*
Luke 19:10

Fireproof Faith that is intentional is deliberate and purposeful, clearly visible, and always in the moment. It is present, it requires you to do the necessary work to sustain your faith and show up every day. This is essential if you are going to be successful in living a life that is filled with intentional fireproof faith for every season of life. In our continuous pursuit for a closer relationship with Jesus Christ, we must realize that we make daily decisions that either move us closer to or further away from God. This is why it is very necessary to stay in shape, show up and make good decisions. Just as you go to the gym to get in better shape you must exercise fireproof faith and discipline your hearts and minds in the same manner.

Discipline yourself to take the time that is needed to get to know God. *Take time for God.* We are all busy and it's hard to make time to study, pray, fast, etc., but if we do not take the time to get to know God and develop the relationship that He created us for we are living a life that is meaningless. God lives in eternity and is not governed by time, time was created for us. The very purpose of our life, our time, is to glorify the God that created us. It has been said, how we spend our time is what we love and who we are. So who are you? Are you putting in the time to grow your fireproof faith?

Show up, be intentional, God is waiting for you.

FIREPROOF FAITH IS: DILIGENT

"In whom we have boldness and access with confidence by the faith of him."
Eph. 3:12

Diligent, fireproof faith is always consistent and continues to show up, regardless of life's circumstances. Being diligent in faith requires that the believer preservers and remains driven. God desires our faithfulness all of the time. On good days and bad, when life is good and when life seems not to be fair and challenging. To be diligent also requires boldness. It's been said before and still remains true, *faith is a muscle you exercise.* The more you do it, the more confidence you have to do it again. Becoming a person who possesses fireproof faith is an accumulation of small first steps, but you must continue on a daily basis to put your faith in action. Choosing faith over what you feel in your flesh is a daily task and this task must be accomplished. It really is just that simple, so make the choice to continue to be diligent and never stop leaning in even when it seems awkward, does not make sense, and doesn't seem fair. God is seeking those who will trust Him even when it seems that you are being extreme to others and even when others do not accept you or understand you. It is also important to remember that when you are a believer who is diligent in your pursuit of fireproof faith that you are proactive. Proactivity refers to self-initiative, being change-oriented, taking action in advance. In other words, seeing what needs to be done and doing it. Fireproof faith cannot be obtained with a casual attitude, every day must be a day that you set goals to be better than you were the day before. If you were weak in faith today, set a goal to be twice as faithful the next day. Do not allow the enemy to fill you with condemnation and guilt. Building a relationship with Jesus Christ is a journey. The Word of God tells us:

> *"The race is not given to the swift nor the strong but to those who endure."*
> ***Eph. 9:11***

You must continue to serve God, live a life of service helping others, and continue in your pursuit towards fulfilling your God-given purpose. When you set clearly defined faith goals on your journey of building a relationship with Jesus Christ and begin to accomplish those goals, your level of fireproof faith will increase. The more you do the more grow, the more you grow in faith the more God sees that He can trust you. The Word of God states that "God is faithful to those who show themselves faithful." The world has a quote that states, "Hard work or diligence pays off." So be diligent, lean in, and be proactive in your pursuit, in building a strong relationship that possesses Fireproof Faithful.

> *"May we never tire of doing what is good and right before our Lord because in His season we shall bring in a great harvest if we can just persist."*
> **Gal. 6:9**

Carpe Diem!

FIREPROOF FAITH IS: *UNDENIABLE*

Undeniable fireproof faith is something that my husband and I had to possess early in our marriage. Many times, fireproof faith will be tested. You must remain steadfast. My family went through a period like this just before my husband and I were married. We were challenged by Rodney's two major health issues. While we were still engaged, my husband began to experience serious back pain. He went to several doctors and hospital emergency rooms in an attempt to relieve his back pain and find a remedy for his illness. This illness and back pain were unbearably intense for my husband. It became so bad that he could not stand in the shower to bathe and when he tried to stand in the shower, the pain would become so bad that he would pass out while showering. I remember sitting in the living room on the sofa and hearing him fall. He had passed out on the bathroom floor. This was very frightening. I called an ambulance and they rushed him to the hospital emergency room. The doctors admitted him to the hospital to run a battery of tests due to the fall and the back pain. I stayed at night with him and prayed for him, however, I had to leave the next morning early enough to go home and get myself and our son ready for work and school.

While at work I received a phone call from a former friend of both my husband and me. He said he had gone to visit my husband and the doctors told him that they had just received the results from an MRI test. The doctors told him that they had just received the results from an MRI test and they needed to take my husband into surgery within the next few hours to remove an infectious mass on his spine. They needed to remove it immediately because it was beginning to go into his bloodstream. After the very long, intense surgery had concluded the doctors came out and told me and my husband's father that they removed all of the infectious mass from his spinal area. The doctor told me, in a tone that was very negative, that my husband would probably never walk again. Even though the doctor came to me with his report, I was sure that his report would not be the final say regarding Rodney's recovery or life. He stayed in the hospital for many weeks and, during this time, to seemingly add insult to injury, he developed a decubitus ulcer on his upper buttocks due to lying on his back and not being turned every hour by the nursing staff. So, he had to undergo another surgery to remove the ulcer. This required a large portion of skin tissue, and muscle mass to be cut away.

After this surgery, he was sent to a nursing home to recover and receive his first attempt at rehabilitation. This was a very trying time for both of us. I was still working and taking care of my teenage son and visiting and caring for my fiancé at the time. God was truly with us and covering us during this season of our lives. Finally, the doctors decided that Rodney was stable enough to go home and continue his healing process. However, he was still not able to walk. He also and an open wound on his buttocks the size of a grapefruit. We cried and prayed and talked to each other about what we should do and what our next steps should be. We both knew we loved each other… but would love be enough to help us endure what we were facing? What would a future look like for us, given Rodney's health challenges? After much prayer and counsel from a minister we'd both known for years, Rodney asked me to marry him again and I agreed to be his wife. We both knew without a shadow of a doubt that this was God's will for our lives in that season and moving forward.

Our wedding took place in our home and Rodney was still not walking at the time.

After our wedding, our days continued to consist of rehabilitation, home exercise, long rides in the car, talking, praying, reading the Bible, continued to speak faith, laughing, loving, watching movies, board games, believing that Rodney would walk again, and watching TBN.

It was during one of our moments of watching Benny Hinn on TBN that Rodney began to repeat what the man of God said over the television, "I am healed, I can walk." He stood up from the side of his in-home hospital bed with the assistance of his walker and begin to take small steps forward. Praise God!

The small steps of faith that he took on that day have led to larger steps of undeniable fireproof steps of faith in his life and our marriage to this day. This season of our lives had so many other challenges that took place during this time: financial, job loss, naysayers, family and friends' betrayal and so much more. But God was with us through it all! It was not easy then and we still face life challenges just as other individuals and married couples also have in their lives. However, God's hand has been and still remains in our lives and His undeniable manifested power has never wavered. We never doubted that God would ever leave us or forsake us. We held on to what we had been taught in the Word of God and believed that God was faithful to perform what He had done so many times before. My husband was an incomplete paraplegic for eighteen months and he had to learn how to walk again at age forty. Today, he walks and proclaims the Gospel of Jesus Christ. We both have been blessed to pastor and lead *Word Of Life Christian Ministries Church* currently for ten years.

> *"You are the light of the world. A town built on a hill cannot be hidden. Neither do people light a lamp and put it under a bowl. Instead they put it on its stand, and it gives light to everyone in the house. In the same*

*way, let your light shine before others, that
they may see your good deeds and glorify
your Father in heaven."*
Matthew 5:14-16

Webster defines the word *undeniable* as something that
is unable to be disputed or questioned. Unwavering,
unshakeable, fortified.

*"Through faith we understand that the
worlds were framed by the word of God, so
that things which are seen were not made of
things which do appear."*
Heb. 11:3

When a believer has undeniable fireproof faith they
have the kind of faith that calls those things which be
not as though they are. This is the kind of faith that
moves God. Then, there are people who think that this
type of faith is senseless or naive. They say that if you
cannot see something or feel something in the physical
realm then it just does not exist. I say that these type of
people are most miserable. Then there are those who
think they have undeniable faith, or really hope they
have it and really work hard to prove they have it. I say
these people live a life of uncertainty.

However, there are those people or believers who actually have the testimony of successfully living a life of undeniable fireproof faith. They have a true relationship with God, and the revelation of who God is dwells on the inside of them. These are those that the Bible says, do exploits for their God. They live a life of joy, peace, power and operate in the anointing of God. They are filled with the Spirit of God and seek to daily express in word and deed the undeniable fireproof faith that God requires of each of His sons and daughters.

Some say that this is a hard requirement for any human to attain, and I agree it is, however, there is only one way to obtain this type of faith. You must have a true desire to receive it. There is only one person that you can receive this type of faith from and that person is God Himself. God created faith and He is only moved by our faith in Him. Undeniable fireproof faith is a gift. The ability to believe and never doubt is a gift from God through His Son Jesus Christ and there are few who rise to this level of faith.

God knew this and that is why He gives us His faith when our faith is weak or small. Just like the man who cried out to Jesus, ***"Lord I believe but help my unbelief." Mark 9:24***

Our faith alone is not enough to bring us to the level of faith that is required of us. We need the faith of His Son Jesus Christ to attain this high level of faith. The Bible tells us that Jesus is the author and the finisher of our faith. ***Hebrews. 12:2***

So, we can rest in the assurance that God does give us His faith, to a degree into our hearts and minds. This assists us supernaturally in building our most holy faith over time. Faith is a development process and a choice of each individual's respective will. We should understand that both aspects are at work in the life of every true Christian believer.

> *"For by grace are ye saved through faith; and*
> *that not of yourselves: it is the gift of God."*
> ***Eph. 2:8***

The world should be able to recognize that you are a believer by the way you act and the words that come from your mouth. People with Christ-like character should have fireproof faith that is undeniable and fortified. Obtaining this type of faith is a process that comes by successfully entering into and coming out of daily faith fights and challenges victoriously. Further, every test and trial should bring revelation, and the anointing which is the power of God allows us to operate at this level of Faith.

At this level of faith, the faith of the believer is fortified and not easily shaken or penetrated. At this level of faith, the believer is not moved by everything that someone says, does, or does not do. At this level of faith, the believer will be faced with greater challenges. In fact, you're in a life-and-death battle for your faith. Satan is determined to shipwreck and destroy your faith. The stronger your faith, the greater his attack will be against it.

You see, fortified faith in Jesus Christ causes hell to rage. Nothing poses a greater threat to Satan's kingdom than a believer who is unshakeable in their faith. Why? Because it is by faith that the power of Satan's kingdom is destroyed. Through fortified, undeniable fireproof faith, Satan's fiery darts have no effect and God's promises are obtained and every weapon and lying tongue that forms shall not prosper.

> *"Every God-begotten person conquers the world's ways. The conquering power that brings the world to its knees is our faith. The person who wins out over the world's ways is simply the one who believes Jesus is the Son of God."*
> ***1 John 5:4***

This type of faith is a gift from Jesus Christ. Those who possess it are truly blessed by God. This type of faith cannot be hidden and should not be hidden. This type of faith touches the heart of God and cause Him to move on our behalf. Finally, this type of faith is visible in the life of the believer. It does not have to be introduced, it shines from within. So, how bright is your faith?

This little light of mine,
I'm gonna let it shine
Let it shine, Let it shine, let it shine!

CHAPTER 7

THE SPIRIT OF AGREEMENT

*That they all may be one; as thou, Father,
art in me, and I in thee, that they also may
be one in us: that the world may believe
that thou hast sent me. And the glory which
thou gavest me I have given them; that they
may be one, even as we are one: I in them,
and thou in me, that they may be made
perfect in one; and that the world may
know that thou hast sent me, and hast loved
them, as thou hast loved me.*
John 17:21-23

*"Again I say to you, if two of you agree
on earth about anything they ask, it will
be done for them by my Father in heaven.
For where two or three are gathered in my
name, there am I among them"*
Matt. 18:19-20

The definition of *spiritual agreement* as given to me by the Holy Spirit is a state of mind, a way of thinking, in which people share the same opinion, or thought about a specific topic, belief, or moral idea.

The dictionary definition of a promise is a spoken or written agreement to do or not to do something. The dictionary definition of a covenant is a sacred or religious agreement, between God and mankind. Covenants make known God's spiritual promises. This lets us know that the covenants and promises of God are conditional. Throughout the Bible, God demonstrated to mankind if they would keep His covenant, He, God would also keep His covenant/ spiritual agreement with mankind.

The Bible tells us about the event that took place on Mount Sinai. This is where God reminded the people of Israel that He had chosen them and was giving them commandments and laws that would guide their relationship together. The agreement was such that, Israel promised to obey the Lord's laws and worship Him only. The *spiritual agreement* was sealed when Moses sprinkled blood on the people and on an altar. This occurrence can be found in, the book of ***Exodus 24***. If the people had obeyed this agreement and continued to be faithful to God, they would have received the blessings of God. If they disobeyed God's law and worshiped other gods, they would be punished. This occurrence can be found in the book of **Deuteronomy 4**.

Just as fireproof faith is a requirement for the believer on their spiritual journey, the spirit of agreement must be a part of every believer's life. Faith that is aligned and in agreement with the will of God activates God's favor, provision, and protection. Again, this spiritual law is very powerful in the life of the believer, however, the *spirit of agreement* applies to the just and the unjust. How and why can this be you ask? Because, when people are in agreement with the will of God, God is obligated to respond to His Word. Words are powerful. The Word of God admonishes us to be careful of what we say and speak out of our mouths.

"Death and life are in the power of the tongue, and those who love it will eat its fruits."
Prov. 18:21

"Whoever guards his mouth preserves his life; he who opens wide his lips comes to ruin."
Prov. 13:3

When you speak the Word of God in faith and agree with the Word of God, all of heaven stands at attention and waits for the command from the Father to act and move on our

behalf. When Jesus was here on this earth, He did only what He heard the Father speak and tell Him to do. This is why we as believers must always say and speak what God says, believe what God believes, and hate what God hates. This is how we live by and embrace the law of spiritual agreement. The spirit of agreement, according to the Word of God says this: If I speak and agree with someone, and we then pray in FAITH, that same agreement in the spirit realm, according to the Will of God. The Father will give us exactly what we ask of Him in the spirit realm and natural realm.

> *"Can two walk together,*
> *except they be agreed?"*
> ***Amos 3:3***

Agreement is one of the necessary ingredients in natural and spiritual relationships. Many people begin natural intimate relationships, without understanding the importance of this spiritual law. Many couples assume before marriage that they agree about various aspects of natural relationships.

However, they never really talk, listen, or ask the other person's perspective or expectation regarding very important relational matters before entering into business partnerships, or marriage. The spirit of agreement is so very important and necessary before anyone should even begin to think about entering into an intimate relationship with another person or Jesus Christ. Developing an intimate relationship with God begins with *agreement*. If anyone desires a deeper relationship with God you must come into agreement with His Word His will and His way.

> *"I have hidden your word in my heart that*
> *I might not sin against you."*
> ### *Psa. 119:11*

> *"Your Word is a lamp to my feet and a light*
> *to my path. I have promised that I will*
> *keep Your Law."*
> ### *Psa. 119:105*

CHAPTER 8

THE WORSHIP FACTOR

"As the hart panteth after the water brooks,
so panteth my soul after thee, O God."
Psa. 42:1

True worship towards God requires
relationship, if there is no relationship,
then there is no revelation from God and no
access into the presence of God. The Bible
states that, "God is Spirit and they that
worship Him must worship in
Spirit and in truth."
John 4:24

W orship by definition is to show strong love and adoration towards something with unquestionable devotion. Therefore, you must know something about the character of the person that you give worship to and have an established relationship with that individual.

In Christianity, worship is the act of attributing reverent honor and homage to God.

The questions that come to the natural mind when given this definition is, why would someone bow down to a God they cannot see, or touch? And why should we worship God and His Son Jesus? I once heard a preacher say "All you need is a memory." If we can stop for a moment and begin to remember all the things in life that we could not achieve on our own and it took God's intervention on our behalf to succeed. If we would stop for just one moment and think about all the things He has done and continues to do, the question would be answered.

The truth becomes evident that we are indebted to God. We as born-again believers now have a relationship with Him because of the confession that we made. We should be able to look back over our lives and also recognize some established history. By history, I mean we can point to or testify and show proof of God working in our life and on our behalf in good and bad times and in challenging situations and circumstances. Our life should testify of God's presence and power in our life. We owe God true worship.

Because He is God, we worship Him. The Bible says:

"Therefore, since we are receiving a kingdom that cannot be shaken, let us be thankful, and so worship God acceptably with reverence and awe."
Heb. 12:28

"Because God commands us to worship His Son Jesus because of the sacrifice He made at Calvary. Worship the Lord your God, and serve him only."
Matt. 4:10

The very fact that we are made by God triggers an innate yearning to recognize honor, offer recognition, and worship Him. We are spirit, soul, and body, and because of this our spirit man places a demand on our natural man or flesh. So don't fight the feeling, when you have the desire to say *thank you* and feel grateful, for all that God has done. Even when there is no one else around but you, don't fight the feeling, your spirit man is doing what it was designed to do, worship the true and living God, the creator of heaven and earth. We should continually be in a posture of worship towards our God.

TRANSACTIONAL WORSHIP & RELATIONAL WORSHIP

Transactional worship is the type of worship that most people engage in. It is the type of worship that treats worship as a transaction. This type of worship is looking to receive rather than humbly give something to God. For individuals who are engaged in transactional worship, their motive is to receive a specific benefit. They feel that if they praise and worship God, He is obligated to give them something in return.

During my research for this writing, I came across an article that explained the difference between transaction and relational worship. Further, I have been a praise and worship leader for many years, therefore much of my own insight as revealed by the Holy Spirit and my personal experience regarding worship is expressed in this writing.

Our God is a God of relationship, and worshiping Him requires relational worship. In relational worship, the worshipper seeks to establish and continue a relationship with who they are worshipping. This type of worship does not seek to receive something from God, the worshipper wants to give something to

God. The worshipper seeks to give their entire being to God in the posture of worship.

> *"Bless the Lord, O my soul: and all that is within me, bless his holy name."*
> **Psa. 103:1**

Transactional Worship and Relational Worship

Transactional Worship is for the benefit of the worshipper, whereas relational worship is for the interest and benefit of God. Transactional worship focuses on external and posture, whereas relational worship focuses on the heart, which may result in some external manifestations. The Bible tells us, in Psalms 47:1, "Oh, clap your hands, all you peoples! Shout to God with the voice of triumph."

Transactional worship follows a prescribed set of rules of formality for worship, whereas relational worship focuses on spiritual relationship and spontaneous action.

> *Hallelujah! Praise the name of God, praise the works of God. All you priests on duty in God's temple, serving in the sacred halls of our God,* **Shout "Hallelujah!"**

> *because God's so good, sing anthems to his*
> *beautiful name.*
> ***Psalm 134:1-3***

In Transactional worship, by its nature as a transaction, the object of worship is distant. On the other hand, in relational worship, the object of worship, God, is personal and is developed and express because of the personal interaction or experience.

Because God is a relational God, he requires His children to stay connected to Him in every aspect of their lives. Therefore, because we have chosen to allow God to direct our lives in every area of our lives we should desire for Him to be involved daily in our lives.

> *"**Abide** in Me, and I in you. As the branch*
> *cannot bear fruit of itself, unless it **abides** in*
> *the vine, neither can you, unless you **abide***
> *in Me. "I am the vine, you are the branches.*
> *He who **abides** in Me, and I in him, bears*
> *much fruit; for without Me*
> *you can do nothing."*
> ***John 15:4-5***

Transactional worship involves the use of formalities that approach the object of worship, whereas relational worship involves the use of past and present interactions with the object of worship, God.

> *Because he holds fast to me in love, I will deliver him; I will protect him, **because he knows my name.** When he calls to me, I will answer him; I will be with him in trouble; I will rescue him and honor him. With long life I will satisfy him and show him my salvation.*
> **Psalm 91:14-16**

Transactional worship most often requires an appointment, time, and place, whereas relational worship takes place anytime and anywhere.

God is omnipotent and He is everywhere in the same place at all times. Our God is not limited by time or space. The Bible lets us know that He will be with us now and even until the end of all ages, so we must live a life of worship towards God. He is a faithful God and does great things for us daily. Daily, He loads us with benefits of health, protection, patience, love, forgiveness, and provision just to name a few. Therefore, there should never be a limit or boundary to the worship that we give to our God.

> *"From the rising of the sun unto the going
> down of the same the Lord's name is to
> be praised."*
> **Psa. 113:3**

Transactional worship does not require the worship to surrender much at all, however, relational worship requires that the worshiper surrender their heart, soul, mind, and strength.

> *"And thou shalt love the Lord thy God
> with all they heart, and with all thy soul,
> and with all they mind, and with all they
> strength; this is the first commandment."*
> **Mark 12:30**

So, check yourself and prayerfully consider whether you are engaging in transactional worship or relational worship. Pray and seek to engage in relational worship, and never be afraid, embarrassed to worship our God who has given everything for us, with your entire body, soul, and Spirit.

> *"Therefore, I urge you, brothers and sisters,
> in view of God's mercy, to offer your bodies
> as a living sacrifice, holy and pleasing to
> God, this is your true and proper worship."*
> **Rom. 12:1**

Worship is Relationship

CHAPTER 9

NATURAL INTIMACY

Natural intimacy... what is it? This category of intimacy deals with human nature and the flesh. It calls for getting to know someone on a physical level—however, intimate relationships are necessary. We must know and understand that the premises of developing natural and spiritual intimacy have similarities. I have learned in my research of this topic that there are four categories of natural intimacy, relationship therapist Alyssa Marie stated in her online article, "What are the 4 types of Intimacy" described intimacy in four categories. These categories are necessary for a natural intimate relationship to be successful and thrive. I chose to provide her perspective and also what God said to me about natural intimacy.

Category #1 Emotional Intimacy

In this category, individuals are affirming, caring, and interested in others' feelings.

Thoughtfully process your feelings before you speak, and when you do speak, summarize your emotions so you can communicate them clearly. Don't rely on qualifiers to cushion your earnest feelings, get right to the root of what you're feeling and be honest and let your mouth speak what your feeling. No filter required, speak the truth in love.

Allow yourself to be vulnerable. When you engage in honest emotional intimacy, it is sometimes very uncomfortable and to be quite honest scary because you don't want to hurt the other person's feelings or make them angry in some instances. However, if you desire to have an emotionally connected relationship you must allow yourself to be vulnerable. You must know that there is risk involved, risk of your feelings being hurt and risk of hurting the other individual feelings. Not to damage or destroy, but to get to the root of the matter and move forward in a positive direction.

Category #2 Mental Intimacy

Consider mental intimacy as a meeting of the minds. Meaningful conversation, shared values, and interest.

Mental intimacy—it's satisfying, it's challenging and stimulating. I found this category to be so true and relevant in my own personal experience and relationship with my husband. Before we were intimate partners and husband and wife, we were friends. When we were dating, we enjoying talking and discussing a myriad of topics. We discussed our dreams,

future goals, regrets, and fears. We would talk on the telephone for hours, sometimes our telephone batteries would actually run out of power during these most meaningful conversations. This is what helped us to connect and bond on a mental level. We still practice this category today after sixteen years of marriage. We also found that by engaging in this way our relationship was stimulated and invigorated and strengthen.

"Iron sharpeneth iron; so a man sharpeneth
the countenance of his friend"
Prov. 27:17

Category #3 Physical Intimacy

Being physical is defined as or having to do with or relating to the body as opposed to the mind, tangible, or concrete. Physical intimacy is characterized by physical attraction or romantic love, sexual activity, or other passionate attachment. This type of intimacy is common and natural within the natural realm.

Just as a child must bond to their mother and father after birth. It is also important for adults who are involved in a marital relationship to bond on a physically intimate level. God designed us this way, so we should not fight against it or be uncomfortable talking about it. Satan desires to distort and cause something that God created to be shared between a husband and a wife to become shameful. The Bible says, in **Hebrews 13:4**, *that marriage honorable in all, and the bed undefiled.*

It is important to know and understand that no meaningful relationship can survive without intimacy. Intimacy at every level is the foundation of any successful relationship, and without it, a relationship will unfortunately fail. Human beings both male and female require intimacy but require communication and contact with one another, otherwise, we are just interacting robotically and lack the ability to socially interact with one another.

This type of behavior is enacted and also taught throughout our childhood and adolescence. It involves being open and talking through your thoughts and emotions, letting your guard down (being vulnerable), and showing someone else how you feel and what your hopes and dreams are. We must listen, trust, and feel another person's heart without placing our own ideas in the mix. True intimacy is a matter of the heart and is acquired over time, and it requires patience and effort from both partners to create and maintain a healthy, solid relationship.

God's plan for mankind was to be in relationship with His creation in a very intimate way. The four categories that are associated with natural intimacy, foster closeness and connection and are a matter of the heart. It is my observation that developing spiritual intimacy between God and mankind is very similar to natural intimacy. It is my perspective the most important of these four categories is spiritual intimacy.

Category #4 Spiritual Intimacy

This category deals with respect for each other's beliefs, shared purpose, nurture each other inner peace.

Spirituality can take different forms or expressions. It could be a code of values or ethics, versus using actual spiritual language or practices.

It has been through my personal experience that spiritual intimacy should be considered prayerfully before entering into a personal or marital relationship. Because we are all individuals and have different world views due to our upbringing, it is important to discuss, understand, and agree on the spiritual beliefs that will guide your relationship. By not doing this we may experience confusion, disagreements, and heartache. Spiritual intimacy with another individual is extremely important and should not be entered into ill-advisedly. On this level, it is important that your values, moral standards, and religious belief are compatible. I have heard of couples who do not have similar or the same religious beliefs that say that they are happy and respect one another's differences, however, the question that comes to my mind is, how are you in agreement? For believers, the Word of God should always be the "Spiritual Authority" that guides a relationship. The Bible says this, *"Can two walk together, except they be agreed?" **Amos 3:3***

My husband and I chose to have spiritual marital counseling before we became husband and wife. During one of our sessions, we had the opportunity to express to each other what our spirituality meant to us individually, as well other areas of importance regarding building a successful marital relationship. Building strong spiritual intimacy was the best thing that we could have ever done for our relationship. We both were members of the same church, so some of our spiritual beliefs were similar and some where not. Now that we are married, we still have moments when we do not agree regarding spiritual matters. When we disagree, we talk it over, pray about it, or just agree to disagree and allow God to open our eyes to His will concerning the matter.

CHAPTER 10

SPIRITUAL INTIMACY

S piritual intimacy with God, what is it and how is it attained? Everyone's relationship with God is individual and varies in the way it evolves. Some may say it is hard to accomplish because they can't see God, however, He can be felt, He is attuned with our feelings and emotions and He loves us unconditionally.

The Holy Spirit gave me this definition regarding spiritual intimacy:

Forethought, effort, and constant attention that is given when one is seeking or has a desire to develop a deeper and consistent relationship with one's creator, God. It is God revealing Himself more and more to those who seek Him and believe He is who He says He is. Then, we are learning more about Him over time. Learning to trust Him more and more to the point you allow Him to be the Lord of every area of your life.

During our premarital counseling, my husband and I learned during one of our sessions that marriage is a lifetime of negotiation and compromise. Developing a long-lasting happy relationship is not totally effortless, it requires deliberate forethought and attention. Spiritual intimacy requires the same attention and forethought. It is important to understand and remember that receiving the Lord Jesus as Savior and Lord is only the first step in developing spiritual intimacy with Him. Developing a very real relationship with Jesus Christ is not an automatic thing, as a matter of fact, it is just the opposite. This relationship is built over time and established by many tests, trials, tears, and testimonies.

Acting in a perfunctory manner is one of the things that negate the building of a strong spiritual intimate relationship with Jesus Christ. Perfunctory behavior should not be a character in the life of the believer. What does this mean? Sometimes as believers we begin to do things out of formality even if these things are the "correct" and "Christian Thing" to do.

For example,
- I prayed today
- I went to church
- I fed the poor

However, the pursuit to develop spiritual intimacy with God and know Him more deeply sometimes becomes an afterthought. No matter how long you've been a Christian, you should never allow yourself to become an individual who seeks God in a perfunctory manner. The desire to know God in the power of His might and the power of His resurrection should always be something that one hungers and thirst for. There should always be a need to embrace and desire to have more of God in our lives.

> Not as though I had already attained, either
> were already perfect but I follow after, if
> that I may apprehend that for which also
> I am apprehended of Christ Jesus. Brethren,
> I count not myself to have apprehended: but
> this one thing I do, forgetting those things
> which are behind, and reaching forth unto
> those things which are before, I press toward
> the mark for the prize of the high calling of
> God in Christ Jesus.
> **Philippians 3:12-14**

God created each of us with a longing for intimacy—intimacy with Him. So, innate desire and longing to be in a spiritual intimate relationship with your Creator was placed inside of you before the foundations of the universe. We must come to the realization that we were created for fellowship with our Creator. We need Him and we long to be connected to someone greater than ourselves. The thing that gives me joy is knowing that He desires to be close to us, intimate with us and in fellowship with us daily. Yes! God Himself desires us. The Father gave the very best He had, His only Son to redeem what Adam gave away in the garden. Why did He do this? Because He desired to be in a spiritually intimate relationship with His creation.

Adam and Eve were not alone in the Garden of Eden. They were with God. God not only visited them on a regular basis, but he walked with them in the Garden of Eden. He did not visit Adam and Eve in the Garden of Eden only to issue commands. The Garden of Eden was where he fellowshipped with Adam and Eve. This fellowship was mutually enjoyable, and the Bible says that, "Adam and his wife were both naked, and they felt no shame." However, this relationship changed the day Adam and Eve sinned. God desired and longed to be in a spiritually intimate relationship with mankind once again, so much so that He sacrificed the ultimate gift that we might walk in relationship with Him once again.

The very idea that the Father desires to be spiritually intimate with me makes me blush. I feel so important and necessary in the grand scheme of creation. God loved me before my parents even knew me, He placed His spirit on the inside of me and gave me an innate spiritual desire to long for His plan and His purpose and presence for my life. So much so that, now my own personal desires now fall in line with His Kingdom purpose. This causes the spiritual intimate relationship between us to grow deeper and stronger daily. God has gone to great lengths to be in relationship with His creation. From the time He walked with Adam and Eve until now, God's desire towards us, has not and will not ever change.

What does it take to be in a spiritually intimate relationship with God? This type of relationship only requires that the believer of Jesus Christ has a relentless pursuit to abide and continually grow daily within their personal relationship with the Father, His Son and be led by the Holy Spirit.

> *Falling in love with Jesus*
> *Was the best thing I ever, ever done*
> *In his presence I feel protected*
> *In his presence never disconnected*
> *There's no place I'd rather be.*

You cannot know someone you don't spend time with. Intimacy develops as a result of consistent contact with someone over time. During this time, and sometimes a lifetime, trust is developed, confidence increases, hearts bind together, and individuals become ingratiated to one another. In a spiritually intimate relationship, the recognition of God's love for us and His love extended toward us should also be considered. Daily, God shows up in our lives. When we wake each morning and when we are sleeping, He watches over us. When we are driving our vehicles He protects us from dangers we know of and dangers we do not know of. God is always with us and around us. He is always cheering us on and guiding us. He continually gives us nudges and speaks to us in a still, small voice. He also speaks through others, through The Word of God or sometimes He has to scream the instructions that He is trying to get to us. God's love is unfailing; the love and relationship grows because we know He loved us first and He told us in His Word that He loves us.

"But God commendeth his love toward us,
in that, while we were yet sinners,
Christ died for us."
Rom. 5:8

"For the mountains shall depart, and the
hills be removed; but my kindness shall not
depart from thee, neither shall the covenant

of my peace be removed, saith the LORD
that hath mercy on thee"
Isa. 54:10

*"But God, who is rich in mercy, for his great
love wherewith he loved us, Even when
we were dead in sins, hath quickened us
together with Christ, by grace ye are saved"*
Eph. 2:4-5

The very thought that the Creator of the universe is always thinking about us and we are always on His mind should be very humbling. If we would allow ourselves to let this thought resonate within our hearts and minds daily that Jesus loves me and am I always on His mind, I believe that our hearts would change. When our hearts are open to the love of Jesus Christ, the level of our relationship and spiritual intimacy increases. There are three actions that need to take place in order for spiritual intimacy to take place.

The first action that needs to be taken to cultivate spiritual intimacy:

CHANGE YOUR PERSPECTIVE

The definition of perspective: The way an individual thinks about or views a person or thing. Our human perspective is limited when it comes to seeing things beyond what they are at that very moment in time. I read a quote by Dr. Tony Evans. "If all you see is what you see, you will never see all that there is to be seen." God's perspective is limitless because He is the creator of all things and is omniscient. God has infinite awareness, understanding, insight, and knowledge of the end—*from the beginning.*

If we are to have a true spiritual intimate relationship with God we must know and understand that God's ways are not our ways and His thoughts are not our thoughts. However, He wants to share His perspective, His mind, and His thoughts with us. This can only take place if we allow the Holy Spirit to lead and guide us. God uses everything that we go through in life to lead, direct, and teach us. We may not even realize the test, trial, or challenge is leading, directing, or teaching us anything at that moment. We just know we're going through something challenging. God will reveal the purpose to us later. It may take days, months, or even years to understand how God, in that moment or season of our lives, caused each event to collectively result in a situation that is both beneficial in our lives and glorifies the Lord.

*"All things work together for good to them
that love God to them which are called
according to his purpose"*
Rom. 8:28

Godly perspective changes both our view and our attitudes. If we allow God to change our human perspective to a kingdom perspective, we can and will have an undisputable and undeniable foundation that cannot be shaken. If you make the choice to change your perspective and your life will change for the better!

The second action that needs to be taken to cultivate spiritual intimacy:

CHANGE YOUR HEART

This is a matter of your will. You must yearn for God to change your heart and transform your human heart and desires to His desires for your life. It is in the heart or will that real change must take place. The heart has the power of choice or the ability to originate a course of action. The heart, spirit, and will of man are interwoven.

God gave us His Word and His Spirit and we respond by putting our faith, trust, and confidence in Him. As we develop a deeper spiritual intimate relationship with Jesus Christ, our heart is changed and we develop a new heart. The heart as well as the spirit of a man is the eternal core of man's being. It is only with our hearts that we can genuinely love and worship God. This is why our praise and worship towards God must always generate from the heart, spirit, and will. The Bible says this,

"I the Lord search the heart, I try the reins,
even to give every man according to his
ways, and according to the fruit
of his doings."
Jer. 17:10

"A new heart also will I give you, and a new
spirit will I put within you: and I will take
away the stony heart out of your flesh, and I
will give you an heart of flesh.
And I will put my spirit within you, and
cause you to walk in my statutes, and ye
shall keep my judgments, and do them"
Ezek. 36:26-27

Hear, O Israel: The Lord our
God is one Lord:
And thou shalt love the Lord thy God with all
thine heart, and with all thy soul, and with

> *all thy might. And these words,*
> *which I command thee this day,*
> *shall be in thine heart...*
> **Deuteronomy 6:4-7**

The third action that needs to take place to cultivate spiritual intimacy:

SEEK HIS PRESENCE

The first thing that every believer must realize is that you owe everything to God and can accomplish nothing without Him. Humility is the position and posture you must espouse continually, before even thinking about entering into God's presence. A posture of humility recognizes that God is greater than anything you can imagine. You must acknowledge that, in the sight of God, we are powerless and owe everything to Him. Many believers never really enter God's presence or experienced a truly spiritual intimate relationship with Him because their ego does not allow them to humble themselves before God in this way. They simply go through the motions and allow their ego, flesh, others' opinions, ideas, suggestions, and thoughts to keep them from entering into the presence of God. One example of this is, some, powerful, successful, wealthy people put their faith in their own mind, body to accomplish what they need. Therefore, they are unable to humble themselves to allow God to become number one in their lives and submit their will to Him. All of these things will keep you from flowing in the power of the Gods' Spirit and experiencing the supernatural presence of God.

Seeking God's presence also means communing with Him daily. When you long to experience deeper times with Him, your desires change, and you find yourself continually in a place of communion. What is communion with God? The word *communion* by definition is: To focus on God, converse, talk, often with profound intensity, intimate communication, or rapport as sharing your heart and mind with God in prayer, meditation, solitude: an interchange of sentiments, ideas, expression, and love.

Spiritual intimacy isn't always about being verbal. Deep relationship with God can be built by sitting quietly seeking His presence, reflecting on His goodness and love, and being in and dwelling in His presence. I have found during my times of seeking and dwelling in God's presence that having a notebook nearby to write down the words and thoughts He impresses upon me during our time of communion. These impressions help when I have gone through a dry season or challenges in my life. These impressions help me to remember that God is able to keep me and bring me through every season of my life. God's Word tells us to put Him in remembrance of His Word, and that includes the Rhema words He speaks to us when we are seeking His presence.

> *"Seek ye the LORD while he may be found, call ye upon him while he is near. Let the wicked forsake his way, and the unrighteous man his thoughts: and let him return unto the LORD, and he will have mercy upon him; and to our God, for he will abundantly pardon"*
> **Isa. 55:6-7**

The fourth action that needs to take place to cultivate spiritual intimacy:

DWELL IN HIS PRESENCE

> *One thing have I desired of the LORD, that will I seek after; that I may dwell in the house of the LORD all the days of my life, to behold the beauty of the LORD, and to enquire in his temple. For in the time of trouble he shall hide me in his pavilion: in the secret of his tabernacle shall he hide me; he shall set me up upon a rock*

Psalm 27:4-5

The Dwelling Places of God in the Bible

The Bible tells us about the various places where God revealed Himself to the children of Israel during the time of their mass exodus in the wilderness. He also created His presence as a tangible object that could be carried around and set up in a tent and reside on the outside of man. God did this in an effort to allow the children of Israel to feel and know that they were never without His presence as they traveled through the wilderness. During my research of this topic, I found that there were three sacred tents or Tabernacles erected for the presence of God to be revealed to the children of Israel during the Great Exodus.

The first was a *"Provisional"* tabernacle built at Mount Sinai for the children of Israel's sin, when they erected an idol, the golden calf. It was placed outside of their camp and was called the *"Tent Of Meeting."* The second was called the *"Sinaitic"* tabernacle. God provided specific instructions to Moses for the building of this sacred tent. This sacred tent was placed in the center of the camp. Some say that this was the headquarters of the camp. The third sacred tent was called the "*Davidic*" tabernacle and it was erected for the Ark of the Covenant. The Ark of the

Covenant was also known as the Tent of Meeting. It was in this tent where God revealed Himself. God would meet the children of Israel when the pillar of a cloud would appear at the door of this sacred tent.

The cloud would always rest upon this sacred tent. However, it is said to come down at the door of the tent when Moses would come to seek God for instruction and direction for the children of Israel. The book of Exodus also speaks about the "Tent Of Meeting" being the place where the priests and Levites would come to make sacrifices and atonement.

"And there I will meet with the children of Israel, and the tabernacle shall be sanctified by my glory... And I will dwell among the children of Israel, and will be their God"
Exo. 29:43-45

The Dwelling Place of God In Our Lives Today

Today we do not have to carry the tabernacle or presence of God around in a tent. We have the great pleasure and privilege of carrying His presence on the inside of us daily. Many Christians have been guilty of mistaking a church building as the only place that God's presence resides. This is so far from the truth. God's presence does reside in the building and the church sanctuary, but not exclusively. His Presence is manifested there because *we*, the living breathing, blood-bought, blood-washed, believers evoke and bring His presence there. When we enter the church building and the sanctuary. When Jesus Christ died on the cross and rose from the grave, he left us the gift of the Holy Spirit. That same Holy Spirit now dwells on the inside of everyone who has accepted Jesus Christ as Lord and Savior of their life.

The dwelling place is where you learn and gain more revelation about God and we learn more about ourselves. God shows us who He is and He reveals His purpose a plan for us in the dwelling place. The dwelling place is a place where a supernatural transformation and encounter takes place. God releases His Glory, power, and presence in and on you, your spirit man acknowledges His presence. Your will yields to His will and your desires become His desire. The new men and new women are brought forth as you vocally express an eternal *yes* to God! We are the Church the Ecclesia, called out, set apart, church, and congregation of Jesus Christ. We are spiritual beings, each of us is a place where the presence of God resides and dwells.

> *"And I heard a great voice out of heaven*
> *saying, Behold, the tabernacle of God is*

> *with men, and he will dwell with them, and*
> *they shall be his people, and God himself*
> *shall be with them, and be their God"*
> ### *Rev. 21:3*

So, faithfully trust God and pour out your heart and soul to Him. Position yourself in humility, listen to His voice, hear what He is saying in the moment, speak to Him, tell Him how much you love Him, and tell Him what is on your heart. God reveals Himself to us in this place. We have to make a conscious effort to refocus our attention away from earthly things God wants to be our dwelling place. Dwell, rest and find peace in His presence. When true spiritual intimacy is accomplished, we allow God to unlock the supernatural which opens the door for *relationship* to evolve and His revelation to be released in our lives. This type of spiritual intimacy is only found in the presence of our Holy God.

CHAPTER 11

REVELATION THROUGH RELATIONSHIP PRAYERS

Prayer For Staying Connected

F ather God, we thank you for your love and grace. We thank you for calling us your sons and daughters. Because we are your children we have access to you. Your Word says, "For as many as are let by the Spirit of God, these are sons of God. For you did not receive the spirit of bondage again to fear, but you received the Spirit of adoption by whom we cry out, "Abba, Father" (Rom. 8:14-15).

So we ask that you, Abba Father will give us the strength and mindset to always stay fully connected to the divine love and wisdom of you heavenly Father, by wholeheartedly trusting in you. We will stay rooted in You; we will worship You and surrender our lives to You. We recognize that without You we can do nothing, we are nothing. To You be all glory and all honor, in Jesus' name. Amen.

Prayer For Receiving Supernatural Revelation

Lord, your Word says, "…When He, the Spirit of truth has come, He will guide you into all truth; for He will not speak on His own authority but whatever He hears He will speak; and He will tell you things to come" (John 16:13). So, Lord God, we come with joy knowing that you desire to provide us with Your truth and Your revelation. Father God, we understand and know that this type of revelation is a gift from You. We thank you that you work in tandem with the Holy Spirit to reveal supernatural revelation that reveals Your perfect will for every area of our lives for no matter if it be past, present, or future.

So God, help us to always, embrace what You have placed on the inside of us what is needed to understand and know the mystery of Your kingdom. Help us to allow the Holy Spirit to convey the mystery of Your will and help us to develop Your wisdom and not reject the wisdom of the world. Father we are intentional in your pursuit and sincere in our desire to engage and receive Your wisdom and supernatural revelation. In Jesus' mighty name we do pray. Amen.

Prayer For Developing The Mind of Christ

Father God, You are our God. We thank you for revelation knowledge and for Your truth.

We pray and ask that you would begin to give us your mind and help us to begin to look at life from Your perspective. We seek to desire Your values and not our own, we want to please You and You alone. So Father, as we begin to look into Your Word, allow the Holy Spirit to begin to reveal who You are and help us to find ourselves in you. Father God, we patiently wait on You, change our minds, change our hearts, and transform us so that we begin to become more like you in, heart, spirit, and in our mind. We thank you in advance that we are becoming more like You each day, in Jesus' name it is so. Amen.

I beseech you therefore, brethren, by the mercies of God, that ye present your bodies a living sacrifice, holy, acceptable unto God, which is your reasonable service. And be not conformed to this world: but be ye transformed by the renewing of your mind, that ye may prove what is that good, and acceptable, and perfect, will of God. For I say, through the grace given unto me, to every man that is among you, not to think of

himself more highly than he ought to think;
but to think soberly, according as God hath
dealt to every man the measure of faith.
Romans 12: 1-3

Prayer For Cultivating Your Vertical Relationship

Oh God, as the deer panteth for the water so does my soul longeth after Thee. You alone are my hearts' desire, and I long to worship Thee. Lord God, help us to die daily to self as we seek to cultivate a more meaningful vertical relationship with You, Father God. Let us desire to live for you daily and to show the love of Christ to others and we begin to develop a more intimate relationship with you. We seek to be more spiritual and filled with your Holy Spirit. Let our only objective be to reflect your image more and more each day.

Father God, our desire is to be drawn closer to you, Father never let us lose our desire and longing to be in your presence and to hear your voice. We seek more of you and less of us each day. We say yes to Your will and yes to Your way, all glory and honor we freely give to you. In Jesus' name. Amen.

Prayer For Developing Revelation Through Worship

Lord God, we thank you for reminding us that true worship with You requires relationship, and if there is no relationship, then there is no revelation and no access to Your holy presence. Your Word reminds us that, "God is Spirit and they that worship Him must worship in Spirit and in truth," John 4:24. God, we recognize and understand that we come from you and without You, we can do nothing. Help us Father God to never forget that it is in You that we live, move, and have our very being. Help us to remember to give you worship, honor, and glory with the dawn of every new day. Let us remember to give you worship, honor, and praise when the sun rises and sets each day.

Father, let us never forget all of the things that you do for us and will do for us because you love us even when we do not deserve your unfailing love. Help us to always remember not to worship You in a transactional way but always remind us that our worship towards you must be relational. In Jesus' name. Amen!

Prayer For Embracing the Spirit of Agreement

Father, Your Word declares that if we keep our covenant with you, You will keep your covenant with us. Father, we understand that if we desire to have an intimate relationship with You we have to be in agreement with You, Your will, and Your ways.

Father, help us to hide your Word deep within our hearts so that we will not sin against you. Lord God, we seek more of Thee and less of us daily. Help us to know and understand that your way is not a yoke or a burden, but they are the way to live abundantly. We thank you in advance for helping us to yield to your Word.

In Jesus' name. Amen.

Prayer For Developing Fireproof Faith

Lord God, we declare and decree that we shall continually trust in You, Father God and focus our faith to be diligent, committed, and consistent. Help us to ensure that our character is completely credible, give us the ability to live, teach, motivate and carry out consistent actions of faith when the direction is not convenient, comfortable, or capable of delivering immediate tangible rewards. Father

God, we understand and recognize that faith is the evidence of our guaranteed success and victory in You. We thank you in advance, in Jesus' name. Amen.

Prayer For Developing Spiritual Intimacy

Father God, we desire to continue to seek after you and develop a consistent relationship with You, our Creator. We have been created in Your image and likeness, and we thank you for revealing Yourself to us as we seek to be more spiritually intimate with You daily. We know in our hearts that You are who you have said you are in Your Word and to us individually. Help us to learn to trust You more and more to the point that we allow You to be the Lord of every area of our life.

Father, we long for Your presence, we desire more of You. Reveal Yourself to us in a new and more intimate way. Oh, mighty God, we need you now, reveal Your glory and pour Your Spirit upon us. We worship You and praise You forever. In Jesus' mighty matchless name, amen, amen, and amen!

Prayer For Developing A Desire to Seek & Dwell In God's Presence

Father, in the name of Jesus, I humbly hand over my heart to You, and I say, "Lord, here's my heart, search me and know me, show me anything in my life that is keeping me from being as close to you and dwelling in Your presence. As You reveal to me these things in my heart and in my life, Holy Spirit, show me what You would have me to do. Take out any un-forgiveness and pride in my heart.

Anything I am hanging on to that belongs to You, anything that I have willingly allowed into my life that is not in alignment with You and Your ways, I lay it down at the foot of the cross. I surrender all to You, Lord Jesus. Thank you for taking these burdens, Lord. Thank you for what You did on the cross to set us free from death. In You I have victory! I praise You, Jesus!

Teach me how to remain in your dwelling place, in the secret place of Your presence. Guide me daily and remind me and teach me how to live in this place of Your holy presence. Constantly remind me that You are with me, that You are before me and behind me. Surround me, always with Your presence as I humbly submit my life to you and seek to dwell in your presence always. In Your great name, Jesus, I do pray. Amen, amen, and amen.

CONCLUSION

J esus says that being spiritually connected is like being attached to a vine. You're not going to have any fruitfulness or productivity in your life if you are out there on your own. You've got to stay connected to the source that created you. Just as it is with trees, a disconnected branch can't bear fruit. You do not have the support or the sustaining nutrients that are there to keep you from withering and dying physically. So it is in the spiritual realm, you must stay spiritually connected to God in order to accomplish the purpose he created you to fulfill here on earth. Your purpose, relationship with the Father, and revelatory knowledge of His kingdom's purpose are all interconnected.

It is the hope of the writer that the readers of these pages gain scriptural insight and explanation of principles that bring clarity and understanding. This book was written for the newly saved Christian and likewise to believers who have been Christians for many years. To enlighten and bring some clarity regarding the fact that, revelation from God is a gift, privilege, and honor to those who yield their lives wholly to God. To convey the fact that before God reveals Himself to anyone, there are actions that must take place. Faith in God, repentance to God, confession to God, belief in God, and commitment to God.

Many of the young adults and even older adults that I have counseled, ministered to, and led during my time in ministry, are not aware of the foundational principles of developing a revelatory relationship with God. Because we live in a world where everyone wants everything immediately, I've found it necessary to share my experience and revelation on this topic. There have been other writings that have attempted to explain this subject. However, God revealed to me that He wanted me to put this specific perspective into the earth for this dispensation and this season. Because we are currently in a time and season of revelation, in which God is revealing and availing truth and direction to the believer and unbeliever of Jesus Christ.

Finally, it is the writer's hope that the reader will have learned that, spiritual intimacy can only occur when we make a conscious effort to refocus our attention away from what is temporal, worldly, and secular. God wants to be our dwelling place and He desires to have a true and meaningful relationship with His creation. When true spiritual intimacy is accomplished, we allow God to unlock the supernatural which opens the door for relationship to evolve throughout our journey of growing in a relationship with God. Then it can be said that revelation through relationship is realized and released in our lives for the enhancement of the kingdom of God.

ABOUT THE AUTHOR

Cornelia C. Armstrong is a wife, mother, co-pastor, worship leader, sister, friend, former college instructor, and author. She is a born again, Holy Spirit-filled believer of Jesus Christ for over thirty years. She loves seeing souls come to know the Lord Jesus as their personal Lord and Savior. Cornelia has faithfully served and assisted in planting other ministries, before her call to serve and lead as co-pastor of Word Of Life Christian Ministries Church. She steadfastly assists and stands with her husband, Pastor Rodney L. Armstrong, who is the Founder and Pastor of Word Of Life Christian Ministries Church.

Cornelia completed a B.A. Degree in the area of Management and Organizational Development and also completed an M.A. Degree in the area of Human Resources Development. She is a sincere and faithful woman of God, who is quick to lend a listening ear and a helping hand. As the Director of the Resilient Women of Virtue at WLCM, Cornelia models the servant leader principle in passion and by example.

Her heart is devoted toward encouraging, inspiring, and empowering the women of WLCM to be resilient women of God. To embrace the purpose that God has placed in each of them individually, for the expansion of the kingdom of God.

REFERENCE

- Bible
- Scripture quotations: KJV
- Holman Bible Dictionary
- Copyright 1991 Holman Bible Publishers
- Pete Bumgarner Ministries - Vertical Relationships
- Nina Keegan – Stay Connected
- The Apostolic Church International - Engage in Relational Worship as a Total Worshipper
- Alyssa Mancao Wellness - Types of Intimacy

CPSIA information can be obtained
at www.ICGtesting.com
Printed in the USA
LVHW020030120222
710698LV00013BA/415